# Summer of Salvia

# Summer of Salvia

### Exploring nature's most powerful hallucinogen and the fabric of existence

## Jason Cole

Copyright © 2017 Jason Cole

All rights reserved.

No part of this book may be used or reproduced in any manner whatsoever without written permission from the author. To seek permission, email the author at summerofsalvia@gmail.com.

Published in the United States by Jason Cole.
www.summerofsalvia.com

Excerpts from Wikipedia.com and Wiktionary.com are licensed under a Creative Commons ShareAlike 3.0 Unported License.

Excerpt from "Get Laid or Die Trying: The Field Reports" by Jeffrey Allen used with permission from the author.

Paperback ISBN 978-1-64136-907-7
Hardback ISBN 978-1-945604-22-5
Ebook ISBN 978-1-945604-33-1

Jacket design by Amygdala Design
www.amygdaladesign.com

First Paperback Edition

# Author's Note

Everything in this book is more or less true. Names have been changed to protect people's privacy, including the name of the author. Some details, like specific locations that might reveal someone's identity, have also been changed, but not in a way that significantly alters the meaning of the events portrayed.

Basically, take this book for what it is—the recollection of my life as it led me into salvia's arms, with a few details changed here and there so my friends and colleagues won't realize what a huge fucking pervert I am.

Introduction

# Introduction

I WENT THROUGH MOST OF MY LIFE AS YOU'VE LIKELY GONE through most of yours: never questioning that the world I experienced every day was real. I took for granted what my five senses showed me every day, blindly believing that the world it showed me was exactly as I experienced it. I took what I saw, heard, felt, smelled and tasted as gospel.

That all changed in the summer of 2009 when, for the first and only time, I smoked *Salvia divinorum*, a powerful, naturally-occurring hallucinogen that forever transformed my view of the world.

I have spent the past eight years questioning everything I thought I knew. I can't trust my senses any longer. Rather than dismiss my salvia trip as a hallucination, salvia has forced me to consider dismissing *my life* as a hallucination—a mirage that salvia temporarily allowed me to see through.

It's a journey that has led me to explore science, philosophy and religion with renewed fervor. And while it's been fulfilling to learn about different perspectives on human existence and what it means to be alive, the most profound effect of smoking salvia is that it prompted me to reflect on my life itself; to explore my past, the forces that have shaped who I am, and the circumstances that led me into salvia's waiting arms—which is an interesting way to put it, because one of the overwhelming feelings I had while tripping on salvia is that the whole experience was inevitable. Preordained, even. It's not a feeling unique to my encounter with salvia. That sense of inevitability is reported by numerous salvia users—just one of the many mysteries surrounding this ancient and powerful drug.

I invite you to read my story, with the knowledge that it's not quite a memoir, and not quite a hard-hitting investigation. It's a bit of both. The result, I hope, is a more human story than you'd get from a dry exposé, but also more informative than a simple memoir.

If you want to forgo the autobiographical stuff, you can skip right to the part that focuses on salvia itself: its history, its modern use, its effect on the human brain, and all the philosophical and religious implications of what people experience on the drug. Start by reading my own experience with salvia, which I describe in the chapter titled "Salvia" on page 121.

As you read about my escapades involving sex, drugs and alcohol (no rock and roll, unfortunately), keep in mind that just because I'm *writing* about all these things, it doesn't mean I'm *endorsing* them, or suggesting you follow in my footsteps. A lot of the shit I've done in my life has been incredibly, deeply stupid. As they used to say on TV: "Don't try this at home." Follow my lead at your own risk.

And if you ignore my advice and decide to try *Salvia*

# INTRODUCTION

*divinorum*, take great caution. Never smoke salvia alone—always have a sitter actively watching you to make sure you're OK until you're done tripping. Although it's rare, it's not unheard of for people to move around while under the drug's effects. Some have even fallen to their deaths.

Stay safe, and thank you for reading my book. I hope, if nothing else, it makes you take a second look at the world around you.

—Jason Cole

# Boyhood Innocence

All of this has happened before, and it will all happen again.
—Disney's Peter Pan

"Salvia? You have salvia?"

It was a warm summer night and there were about ten of us mingling on the deck.

I didn't know any of these people. It was my friend Katie's birthday party and I'd only come to wish her well and drop off her gift. But I'd had a little too much to drink, and the alcohol (mixed with a few puffs of weed) had overridden my normally reserved personality, allowing me to socialize with people that half an hour ago had been—and in a few hours would once again be—complete strangers.

I had returned from a beer run when I heard her mention salvia. I don't remember her name, but I remember exactly what she looked like. She had light brown skin and a long, petite body. Her hair was cut shorter than mine, and for good reason—she

## Summer of Salvia

was in the Army, and she was a lesbian. And, apparently, she was into drugs.

I'd first heard of salvia in my local newspaper. Since I'd just recently started smoking pot, the headline for an Associated Press story by Andrew Bridges sparked my interest: UNPREDICTABLE HALLUCINOGEN IS LEGAL—FOR NOW: PLANT IS SOLD LEGALLY ON THE INTERNET.

The article talked about the plant's use in rituals by an Indian tribe near Oaxaca, Mexico and explained that it wasn't governed by any federal laws "even though, by weight, the active component of salvia divinorum is more powerful than that found in peyote, psilocybin mushrooms or any other natural hallucinogen . . . The drug's effects last anywhere from a few minutes to an hour and more. During that time, users can lose all perception of reality."

This sounded too good to be true! Stories of LSD trips had always fascinated me and I'd always wondered what it would be like to try it.

But I'd also heard stories about people wallowing in bad acid trips for hours at a time, or being plagued by acid flashbacks for the rest of their lives. It was enough to keep me from ever even trying the drug. My reluctance to try "magic mushrooms" stemmed from similar concerns: someone told me that prolonged use burned lesions in people's brains. It was only after a friend convinced me, after weeks of heated debate, of marijuana's relative safety that I gave into peer pressure and smoked my first bowl of weed. But no amount of peer pressure could convince me to try something that could permanently cost me my sanity.

But here was a hallucinogen that only lasted at worst an hour, but probably only a few minutes. Best of all, it was legal.

Of course, I conveniently ignored other parts of the article.

It quoted clinical neurobiologist Dr. Ethan Russo, who said, "I don't know anyone who has ever taken it and said, 'Gee, that was fun,'" and, "It's not pleasant in anyone's conception that I have ever spoken with."

It's not like the guy was saying, "This stuff will kill you!" or, "Salvia kills brain cells!" He was just saying it was unpleasant. If it turned out unpleasant, oh well. I could live with that. As soon as I finished the article, I knew I wanted to try this drug. I had to.

But I was a broke college kid counting pennies, and when I went online to try to buy some salvia, I found out it wasn't particularly cheap (relatively speaking—remember, I was broke, and shipping costs made it more expensive). It was more cost-effective to buy a forty-sack of weed than it was to buy a vial of salvia. Life went on and in time I completely forgot about salvia.

Until I found myself standing on a crowded deck and heard a butch Army chick mention it.

"Yeah, I've got salvia," she said. Immediately, enthusiastically, she asked, "Do you want to try it?"

I didn't hesitate.

"Yes," I said. "Yes, I want to try it. Right now."

"Awesome!" she yelled and threw her hand up for a high-five. I shifted my beer to my other hand and gave her outstretched palm a hearty slap. "Hang on dude, I'll be right back." She rushed into the house and returned a moment later with a bulging backpack. "Come over here," she said, walking to the opposite corner of the deck. I set down my beer and followed her.

"I've always wanted to try this," I said excitedly. "I just read about it not too long ago. This is going to be wild!"

"It's pretty amazing," she agreed. "But it's really intense. Sit down." I complied, lowering myself with my back against the rail of the deck and my knees tucked up to my chin. "You might want to take your jacket off. Sometimes people get really hot after they do this."

"I'll be okay," I said. It was a warm night, but a light breeze was keeping me cool.

She seemed okay with that. She unzipped a pocket at the front of her backpack and took out a little vial—the salvia extract, she explained.

She unzipped the center pocket and pulled out the largest bong I have ever seen in my life. If she'd set it down beside her, it would have stood past her kneecaps.

"Holy shit! That's a huge bong!"

She laughed. "Yeah, this is my baby." Carefully, she unscrewed the vial and tapped some of the extract into the bowl.

Two other people came over to watch me. One was a guy I hadn't talked to yet. I glanced at him and a flash of jealousy shot through me. His T-shirt clung to tanned, defined pectoral muscles and his flawless face was crowned by a perfect head of hair. He was a sharp contrast to me, with my slight beer gut popping out of my shirt and my hair marred by half a dozen cowlicks. It consoled me a little when I found out he was gay—as were most of the people attending the party, it turned out. The other spectator was a cute brunette girl with shoulder-length hair I'd talked to earlier about her bisexuality and her job at a local hardware store.

It gave me a rush to have them watch. They were paying attention to me. I was doing something they were too scared to do. I was *cool* to them. It was a wonderful feeling and I decided right then and there everything I'd been told in school about drugs not being cool was a lie.

She placed the bong between my legs.

"Here's what's going to happen," she said. "You're going to put your mouth over the bong and suck in the smoke. That's all you have to do; I'll light the bowl. Hold the smoke in as long as you can."

"Okay," I said. This was going to be easy. I wasn't a total pothead, but I'd had enough experience smoking weed that I could hold in smoke until my lungs ached, and then some.

I wrapped my lips around the bong. She brought her lighter's flame to the bowl.

"Suck," she said as flame met extract. I sucked in the smoke, filling the air with a bubbling gurgle as the bong water rippled. After what seemed like at least a full minute, she told me to stop. I held my breath. And held it. I became lightheaded.

"Whoa, look at him!" the brunette girl said. "How long can this kid hold his breath?" That gave me quite the ego boost (ironic, since I'd be experiencing an ego death in a few short minutes) and gave me the strength to hold my breath even longer.

Finally, I felt that if I held in the smoke even a second more I'd pass out, so I exhaled. A thin stream of smoke sailed out of my mouth. It looked like it was flowing in slow motion.

I felt a tingling sensation in my right thigh. And although my head felt a little funny and I was seeing stars, the only thing out of the ordinary was this tingling sensation. I thought, *is this it? Is this what all the hype is about?*

That's when shit got crazy. That's when my perception of life, the universe and reality was torn inside out.

Not for five minutes. Not for an hour.

Forever.

I NEVER THOUGHT I'd do drugs. Who actively thinks that early in their life? No one grows up thinking, "Someday, I'm going to put all kinds of substances in my body that will fuck up my perception of the world!"

I've asked myself many times how I got to the point that I found doing drugs acceptable. How did a good, innocent, Christian boy become a booze-guzzling, reefer-smoking miscreant eager to sample a hallucinogen whose effect on the human brain scientists are only now beginning to study?

To answer that question, we must travel back in time a bit. We have to look into the soul of a young boy who is almost unrecognizable to me today.

As a young boy, I was timid, but full of ambition. I was shy, hesitant, and lacked confidence, but I was determined to shed those traits and trade them for those possessed by the heroes I saw every day in Disney movies. I would be as confident and self-assured as Aladdin, as heroic and loving as Pongo, as adventurous and daring as Pinocchio.

That wasn't all. Those were perfectly good and respectable traits for any boy to have. But I didn't want to be just good or respectable. I wanted to be *righteous*.

I realized I would never lead a perfect life—I was told that the only one to ever do that was Jesus Christ—but I wanted to live my life as perfectly as I could. Thanks to my Christian upbringing, I formulated a mental checklist constantly running in the back of my mind. Some of these items only appeared as I grew older. Others evolved as my understanding of the world matured.

- No having sex until marriage
- No watching pornography
- No drinking alcohol (alcoholism runs in my family, so I decided rather than drink in moderation, I would abstain completely—why tempt fate?)
- No smoking cigarettes
- No taking drugs

## Boyhood Innocence

I wasn't raised by religious zealots. Both my parents were Christians and took my brother and me to a Presbyterian church off and on, but, since it was an hour commute, we didn't make it every Sunday.

When we did make it to church, I took what I heard about God, Jesus and the Bible very seriously. I understood that the pastor preaching to me was talking about the very foundation of the universe I inhabited. God created everything I was experiencing through my five senses and, moreover, created *me*. He created my ability to be aware of the world around me. He created my ability to be aware of *myself*. That blew me away. I was fascinated by the concepts of sentience and consciousness. What a wonderful gift to be self-aware! How blessed I felt to be born a little boy instead of a rock or a leaf that couldn't do anything but sit there, never even aware of its own existence.

But the pastor didn't stop there. At some point, obviously, I learned about Jesus Christ, how He died for my sins so I could live with Him forever and ever in heaven. I would never die, because Jesus died for me. All I had to do was believe in Him.

So how could I ever hope to face Jesus Christ in heaven above if I was a womanizing, smut-loving boozehound? The very notion of my savior's disappointment (not his rejection, because I knew Jesus loved me no matter what) filled me with dread. So I wouldn't disappoint him.

It would be like a test, I decided. I might not get a perfect score, like Jesus had, but I would do well and maybe get eighty or ninety percent. I'd show I'd made an effort, that I'd earned my salvation more than the poor saps getting F's. I imagined myself growing up to be the ideal human male. I imagined myself growing up to become President of the United States of America—and my campaign would be the most successful since George

Washington's, because I'd have lived a life of honesty, purity and virtue that set me apart from all other politicians. I would abstain from the pitfalls ensnaring all the competition. No premarital sex. No alcohol. No drugs. I'd decided to become Straight Edge* before I'd even heard the term.

It's funny how life never goes how you plan for it to go.

Looking back, I think my plans were foiled by what I've referred to as shyness, social anxiety, or social ineptitude. Let's just put it this way: I was a terribly awkward little boy.

It's hard to pinpoint exactly when my awkward behavior began, but if memory serves, I'd say it all started in preschool.

It wasn't even a significant event, although it seemed significant to me at the time. What's significant to a child is never the same as what's significant to an adult.

My brother Tim and I went to the same preschool class. I never hesitated to yell at him if he bothered me. We were brothers; politeness was unnecessary.

My brother and I, along with half a dozen other kids, were on the floor one day, playing with some toys when I felt somebody brush up against my leg. I thought it was my brother. "Knock it off!" I yelled. The assault on my leg continued. "Knock it off!" I yelled again. Still the onslaught continued and finally I whipped around and shouted right in my brother's face: "KNOCK IT—"

Only, it wasn't my brother. It was a chubby blond boy, someone I barely knew, and suddenly my confidence evaporated and my voice became small. ". . . off."

I was embarrassed. I had just yelled at a complete stranger.

---

* From Wikipedia: "Straight Edge refers to a lifestyle and youth movement that started within the hardcore punk subculture whose adherents make a lifetime commitment to refrain from drinking alcohol, using tobacco products, and taking recreational drugs. The term was coined by the 1980s hardcore punk band Minor Threat in the song 'Straight Edge.'"

Yelling at my brother was one thing. We were comfortable with each other. But here was someone I barely knew, and I had *yelled* at him!

Looking back, I wonder if I would have developed more self-confidence if that had never happened. Maybe I would have made more friends and developed better social skills. Maybe I would have felt comfortable in my own skin instead of turning to drugs and alcohol. Maybe I never would have done salvia and my life wouldn't have spiraled even further into the depths of mental illness. On the other hand, maybe it was inevitable, just the catalyst opening the floodgate. Maybe my social anxiety is genetic; both my parents are somewhat shy introverts. What matters is that, whether it was nature or nurture that caused it to happen, *it happened.*

That incident set a precedent of awkwardness and social incompetence that followed me all the way through high school. Screw it, let's be honest. To this day, it still hasn't completely lost my scent.

Things weren't any better in kindergarten. We all brought bag lunches from home and ate them at a round table in the classroom. One day, as we were eating, a girl sitting across from me turned to her friend and asked what she had brought for lunch. She smiled devilishly and said, "I'm eating a snake sandwich!"

The air suddenly filled with "ewwws" and "icks," but also with fervent giggling. Honestly, the notion of a snake sandwich grossed the hell out of me, and I didn't find it funny. But I was trying to fit in, so I laughed along with everyone else.

"I have beetles in my sandwich," another girl said. More smiles, more giggles.

"Oh yeah? Well I have *worms* in mine!" said the boy next to me.

Just like that, everybody's lunch was suddenly grotesque and instead of vomiting in revulsion, like I was on the verge of doing, they giggled with their mouths full, crumbs cascading out of their mouths and landing unnoticed on the tabletop. I realized if I wanted to fit in I would have to think of something gross to be eating, and quickly, before every conceivable culinary atrocity had already been picked.

"Well," I said, "um . . . my sandwich is made out of *guts*!"

The laughter stopped. The smiles turned to frowns. The girl that had started this disgusting exchange turned to me and said plainly, "That's *gross*." She said it without giggles. She said it with a tiny hint of malice.

I finished eating my sandwich in silence, barely able to keep it down now that all I could think about were snakes and worms and guts. *How is eating guts any more disgusting than eating snakes or beetles?* I thought. *What am I doing wrong? Why can't I fit in?*

We had two kindergarten teachers, Mrs. Paul and Mrs. Grey. Often, Mrs. Paul directed the entire class to gather on the floor around her. She sat in a plastic chair and read us books, holding them up so we could see the pictures. The stories enthralled me. This is when I decided I loved stories and books.

But when Mrs. Grey pulled us aside individually so *we* could read to *her*, my blood became hot. I saw my peers slowly learning how to sound out letters, then how to string the letters together to form words, and then how to string those words together to form sentences.

I couldn't do it. The first couple times I tried to read the words, I failed horribly, and the sting of those defeats shamed me. It shouldn't have. I'm sure the teachers were very understanding. But every time Mrs. Grey pulled me aside to read to her, the thought of failing again mortified me.

Instead of trying extra hard to learn to read, I paid rapt attention to Mrs. Paul when she read to us. I memorized the books and when Mrs. Grey pulled me aside to read to her, I recited the book from memory. At least, I think I did. To this day, I'm not sure whether I successfully fooled her or not. Maybe she was on to me but didn't want to devastate my self-esteem any more by letting on that she knew.

Writing out words was even harder. If I couldn't recognize a word when it was already constructed, how in the world was I supposed to construct one myself?

But I kept trying. One day, sitting at a table with a blank piece of paper and a red marker, I attempted to write out the sentence: "The car is green." My hand moved the marker across the page, forming the letters and praying I'd arranged them in the correct order. But I was certain, deep down in my heart, that I couldn't possibly have spelled it correctly. I was certain I'd failed then just as I'd failed many times before.

A paraeducator sat next to me helping another student. I turned to her and said despondently, "What does this say?"

She turned to look at my writing and said matter-of-factly, "The car is green."

My breath grew short. I brought the paper up to my face and stared at it. *I wrote this*, I thought reverently. I could hardly believe it. I had taken a bunch of letters that, separately, meant nothing, and arranged them in such a way that they meant something. I had created something out of nothing, honoring God through this tiny imitation of His creation of the universe.

That was the beginning of my love affair with reading and writing. My sudden success was a shot of confidence, but it was an isolated shot. I never excelled at mathematics or history or sports. But when it came to reading and writing, it was like a light bulb suddenly went off in my head. One moment, I couldn't do it at all; the next, I lived for it.

It was the worst thing that could have happened to me.

Giving an introverted boy a book is like giving a schizophrenic person LSD. It doesn't help anything; it just causes them to delve deeper and deeper into fabricated realities. It's nothing more than a means of escaping the world, a way of forgetting that you don't know how to talk to the other kids, you don't know how to play with them the same way they play with each other and you'll never attain the close friendships you long for. Reading, for lonely introverts, is nothing more than an emotional and mental painkiller. It treats the symptoms, not the disease.

As a result, my social skills never reached their full potential. Throughout elementary school, when other kids played on the seesaw, pushed each other on the swings, or played touch football, I parked myself on a bench and immersed myself in a book. It's funny; I remember hardly any of them now. I regret many things about my childhood, but my foremost regret is that I interacted with books more than I interacted with my peers. Middle school wasn't much different. Although I tried harder to make friends, with some success, I still spent more time by myself, usually reading or writing, than I did joking around and playing games and being a normal pre-teenager. It didn't help that I had an unhealthy obsession with science fiction, which eventually developed into a fascination with accounts of UFO abductions. One day I posted a flyer on our class bulletin board, advertising myself as a UFO investigator, asking anyone who had encountered any unidentified flying objects to contact me. One of my classmates came up to me and told me he'd been abducted and anally probed. Then he laughed in my face. I wanted to punch the bastard and wipe the smug grin off his face. If I hadn't had Jesus in my heart, I might have.

There was one notable exception to my solitary middle school existence, and it coincided with the decline of the moral checklist I'd carried ever since I was a little boy. In the sixth grade, near the end of the school year, I snagged myself a girlfriend.

Actually, it was more like she snagged me. For a pubescent boy with an ever-growing interest in the female anatomy, this was dangerous territory.

Every year the sixth-grade class took a weeklong trip to a former military base that had been converted into a campground. It was like a summer camp we got to go to during the school year. We ate our meals in a mess hall, slept in barracks, walked trails, combed the beach, captured each other's flags. Regardless of my anemic social skills, it was some of the most fun I've had in my life.

We had a dance the night before we left. I heard they were going to have a student DJ, and I wanted the job. For some reason, I thought it would blow the other kids away that I was choosing the music they were dancing to. I imagined them coming up to me after the dance and giving me high-fives: "Way to go dude! The music was awesome!"

As a shy person, I spent a lot of time thinking to myself. I spent much of this time inside my own head praying to God. Literally every day, I prayed for a girlfriend. But that night, I abstained from that particular prayer just long enough to make another one: *Please, Lord, let someone ask me to be the DJ for this dance.*

My jaw dropped when I was approached by Travis Epsom, one of the more popular kids in our class, and he asked me if I wanted to be the DJ.

*Holy crap*, I thought. *If this isn't proof that there's a God in heaven, then there isn't any.*

## Summer of Salvia

I accepted. It was only later that I suspected the reason he asked me to be the DJ was because nobody else wanted the job. They wanted to go out on the dance floor and shake their booties. They wanted to go have *fun*, not place CDs in and out of the tray of a CD player. Of course, it still worked out to my advantage, because I felt horribly awkward dancing by myself and the thought of asking a girl to slow-dance mortified me.

As it happened, I wasn't the only one spinning discs. A group of high school students were in attendance serving as chaperones and mentors, and one of them, in possession of a vast collection of CDs, helped me pick out which songs to play. His name was Andrew.

While we sat watching everyone, Andrew told me to go ask one of the girls to dance during the next slow song.

"I can't do that," I said.

"Why not?" he asked with exaggerated incredulity.

"Because," I said. "I'd be way too nervous. I wouldn't even know what to do. And I'd have to ... you know ... *touch her*."

He laughed.

"So? That's half the fun."

I was about to construct a foolproof counterargument when fate intervened.

Maria, a biracial girl who almost always wore her hair in a tight ponytail and always sported a pair of glasses that made her look just a tad bit nerdy (although she never quite achieved the matching reputation, partially on account of her ample bosom) asked me to dance.

I was speechless.

Andrew was more enthusiastic than I was.

"Duuude! Go out there! You're going to have a blast!"

"I ... I, uh ..."

"Go!"

Before I knew what was happening, Maria had grabbed one of my limp arms and dragged me onto the dance floor.

"I, uh . . . I don't really know what to do," I said.

"It's easy," she said. "I'll show you." She grabbed my hands and placed them on her hips. I swallowed heavily. She wrapped her arms around my neck.

"Okay. Um. Now what?"

"Kind of move your feet back and forth like this," she said.

"Okay," I said. I imitated her and gave a little sigh of relief. This wasn't that hard. Still, I couldn't quite get the rhythm down and that made me self-conscious—as did my fervent effort not to develop an erection.

As we swayed back and forth we stared into each other's eyes. It was more of an awkward moment than a tender one, although I suppose there is a sort of mild tenderness to pre-teen inelegance. I turned my lips upward into a smile that was not at all genuine. I wanted to mask my obvious discomfort as much as I could.

Even so, some small part of my brain was elated. *I am dancing with a girl! I am, at this very moment, touching an honest-to-goodness female human being, feeling the warmth of her body against my hands, smelling the sweet fragrance of her perfume. I am close enough to kiss her!* Of course, I was far too self-conscious to gather the courage to so much as peck her on the cheek.

The song ended (I believe it was "Nice and Slow" by Usher) and we released each other.

"Thanks," Maria said softly.

"No problem," I said and scurried back to my seat beside the CD player.

"Dude, that was awesome!" Andrew said when I returned. "Way to go!"

I couldn't help but grin stupidly. No longer in the intoxicating presence of a female, my mind was halfway sober and I let myself reel over what had just happened.

*This is a huge milestone!* I thought. *Maybe this is the start of a social life. Maybe I'll make close friends. Maybe Maria will even be my* girlfriend. *Maybe my luck is about to change.*

I shook my head.

*Not luck. God. He already answered one prayer tonight. And now he's finally answering another.*

I had a feeling—I hoped and I prayed—that Maria would soon become my girlfriend.

# Middle School

The dream is dreaming itself.
—Kalahari Bushmen saying

"Maria likes you."

"Okay..." I said noncommittally.

Maria's friend Heather, a blonde, preppy girl—Maria's complete opposite—looked indignant at my response.

"Well?"

"Well what?"

"Do *you* like *her*?"

"Um..."

I'm sure I seemed mentally handicapped to Heather, like I could barely process her words. In reality, I had processed her words immediately, but they'd sent dozens of other thoughts racing through my mind. I was ecstatic to hear that a girl liked me, of course, and I would have reciprocated the attention of any girl in our class. But the situation was more complicated with Heather delivering the message.

At the start of the school year, Heather had revealed that she had a crush on me. Not verbally, of course. As one would expect from a shy twelve-year-old girl, she wrote me a note asking if I'd be her boyfriend. And, coward that I am, I never even responded to her.

It's not that I didn't want to be her boyfriend. I did. Desperately. Frankly, I wanted to be *anyone's* boyfriend. But I had no idea what, exactly, a boyfriend was supposed to do and I didn't think I'd make a very good one. So I chickened out and, petrified to tell her yes *or* no, I didn't say anything—which probably broke her heart and made me seem like an ass.

But hearts heal quickly in middle school. Not even a week later, Travis Epsom—Mr. Popular—asked her out. They dated for about two weeks, then broke up and promptly started scoping out fresh prospects.

Now here was Heather asking if I liked another girl. She was clearly over the way I'd mishandled her confession of love for me. But I was worried that if I said that yes, I liked Maria very much, Heather would be hurt. She would conclude I'd rejected her proposition because I didn't like her. If I said no, I didn't like Maria, maybe she'd conclude I just wasn't into girls, that I was gay. Some small part of me was so altruistic, so self-sacrificing, that I seriously considered that a better alternative to causing her even the tiniest bit of emotional grief.

"Well do you like her or not?" she asked, exasperated. I had to make a decision immediately.

"Yeah," I said. "I guess so."

I wasn't *that* altruistic.

Heather smiled.

"Okay," she said and ran away, presumably to tell Maria the good news.

Now what was I supposed to do? Ask her out?

I hate to acknowledge my complete lack of balls, but even after hearing that Maria liked me, I was *still* terrified to ask her to be my girlfriend. Some part of me feared this was all an elaborate prank. What if Heather merely told me Maria liked me so when I asked her out, she'd say no and I'd look like a fool? Maybe they were collaborating so Heather could get revenge on me for rejecting her.

Instead of tracking Maria down and asking her to be forever mine, I walked down to the beach to clear my head.

I sat on a log and watched the waves, mesmerized by the way they rolled into the shoreline at an angle. Listening to the waves crash onto shore relaxed me. I felt my breath slow in time with them. When my batteries were fully recharged, I stood and walked back to the campground.

As I made my way to the mess hall for dinner, I ran into Maria and Heather.

"Hi," Maria said smiling.

"Hi," I said. My voice cracked.

"You like each other," Heather said.

*No shit*, I thought.\* But I just nodded.

"Are you going to ask her out?" Heather asked.

"I . . . uh . . ." My face felt hot and sweat dripped off my forehead. "Do you want me to?"

Maria nodded shyly.

"Well, do you . . . do you want to go out with me?"

---

\* Admittedly, it was probably not in those exact words.

"Yes," she said.

"Cool." We stood there for a few minutes, shuffling our legs awkwardly and periodically turning our heads down to investigate our feet.

"Yeah," I said. "So . . ."

It was Heather that finally escalated things; her arm sprung forward and she grasped my wrist. Her other arm gripped Maria's wrist and, not at all gently, she placed our hands together.

The warmth and smoothness of Maria's skin against mine sent chills through my body. It astounded me that holding a girl's hand could have such a profound effect on me. While it had been a long time since I'd been in the habit of holding my parents' hands when we crossed the street, I didn't remember it ever being like this. There was something more going on here than just skin touching skin. Of course, I know now that it was just my wild hormones. But at the time it seemed utterly magical. I understood what people meant now when they said, "there was chemistry between us." I was becoming a chemist. I felt love—not the platonic love I felt for my family, but romantic love, just like I'd seen in movies; just like Aladdin felt for Jasmine, like Pongo felt for Perdita, like Pinocchio . . . well, forget Pinocchio, he was a puppet. The point is, *I was holding a girl's hand! I was holding my girlfriend's hand!* It was incredible. I'm sure my brain bubbled wildly with endorphins.

We only had about an hour left at the camp, but we were inseparable up to the last minute when we loaded our belongings and ourselves onto the bus and prepared for the hour-long drive back to school.

Maria and I sat together on the bus, holding hands. The bus driver turned the radio on to placate the students, and we sang along to tunes like "Sex and Candy" by Marcy Playground and

"Hand in my Pocket" by Alanis Morissette. On the latter song, only a few people sang along, until the line: "I'm sad but I'm laughing, I'm brave but I'm chicken shit." I looked up at the bus driver just in time to see her recoil at the sound of thirty sixth-graders suddenly shouting "shit" in unison.

We rode the rest of the way in silence.

When we pulled up to the school Maria and I hugged each other.

"I'll see you in class tomorrow," I said.

"I look forward to it," she said and she kissed me on the cheek.

I stumbled toward the parking lot in a state of euphoria, lugging my duffel bag over my shoulder and holding my sleeping bag and pillow against my chest as I looked for my parent's car.

Finally, I spotted them. They popped the trunk so I could throw my luggage into it and when I plopped into the backseat I couldn't stop the words that flooded out of my mouth.

"I have a girlfriend now."

"What?!" My mom screamed. "Are you serious?"

"Yeah," I said, grinning.

"Way to go," my dad said with a matching grin. He turned around and stretched his arm into the backseat for a high-five. I slapped his palm timidly.

Then the questions began.

"Who is this girl?" "What does she look like?" "Is she in your class?" "How'd you meet her?" "Did you ask her out or did she ask you?" "You two haven't had sex, have you?"

Normally I would have been embarrassed to answer their questions, but I was in such an elated state that they could have asked me how many times a day I masturbated and I would have earnestly elaborated on every detail.

## Summer of Salvia

At school the next day I spent most of my time in the classroom looking at Maria. It was funny. Before we had started "going out" (which was an ironic term for us to use for dating since neither of us were old enough to drive and we never actually went out anywhere) I'd always thought she was kind of cute, but I'd never been particularly enchanted by her looks. But now whenever I looked at her, I admired the visage of a goddess. I suddenly saw her in a whole new light. Her appearance certainly hadn't changed drastically within the span of a day, but my perception of her had. It's an experience that cemented in me the notion that inner beauty trumps outer beauty. By getting to know someone and developing an attraction to their personality, it's possible for one to appreciate their physical characteristics more. At least, that's the way it seems to work for me. That's the way it worked when I started dating Maria.

Our recesses, which I'd always dreaded as periods of prolonged loneliness, were now an event I looked forward to, because it was time spent holding my dear Maria's hand. I joined Maria as she played games with her friends and, although I was horrible at sports, I tried my hand at kickball, basketball, and tetherball.

Sometimes we'd just lie on the grass holding each other's hands, talking. I don't remember exactly what we talked about. Both of us liked to read—I think it was one of the things that attracted her to me in the first place—so I do remember talking about books. While I was an avid fan of science fiction, she was into horror, a genre I'd never really explored, as I enjoy sleeping at night.

Despite the chemistry that developed between us, I was terrified to kiss her on the lips. We had kissed each other on the cheek a few times, but that was as far as we'd gone.

As the man of the relationship, it was obviously my responsibility to be the bold, daring, confident one. I was supposed to escalate things. That, Hollywood kept reminding me, is what women want. But I knew that would never happen. I was too scared to make the first move. Deep down I hoped Maria would tackle me one day and shove her tongue down my throat. But she never did do that, nor should I have expected her to.

Part of my anxiety over kissing stemmed from the fact that we were never completely alone. I would have been nervous enough kissing her if it was just the two of us. Kissing her while other people watched was unthinkable.

We both lived out in the country, but not near each other. Since neither of us could drive, we had no way to "hang out" after school. We talked on the phone a lot, but that was no substitute for seeing each other in the flesh, for being able to feel the heat radiating from each other's skin and breath.

In fact, I can only recall two "dates" with Maria, if they can even be called that.

On the first occasion, my mom suggested I invite Maria to a movie.

Of course, she didn't think to drop us off and pick us up *after* the movie; that would have been far too thoughtful of her. Instead, she chose to embarrass me by taking Maria out to a movie with my entire family. How was I supposed to work up the nerve to kiss her in the theater if my entire family was there to watch? We dutifully watched the movie, holding hands the entire time but never getting more adventurous than that.

The second occasion was a birthday party for our mutual friend Billy.

Billy was one of the few classmates I'd really connected with. He was a goofy ginger kid, kind of a class clown. He was short and skinny, the latter trait probably a result of hyperactivity—he always ran around, whether in a classroom or a playground.

It was his sense of humor that gave us enough common ground to become friends. I thought he was funny, and I think he appreciated that. We weren't best friends or anything. We didn't hang out all that much outside of school. In fact, the only times I remember ever hanging out with him outside of school were when he came to my birthday party, and when I went to his.

Eventually, all the other kids left and Maria and I were the only ones left. Billy asked if we wanted to walk to get a movie from the video rental store down the street. We agreed and headed in that direction, but at some point we got distracted and ended up sitting and talking on a big log by the side of the road. Maria and I sat there holding hands and after a minute Billy stood and faced us.

"I want to see you kiss," he said.

I laughed.

"Billy, you're a perv."

"I'm not a perv," he said with mock defensiveness. "It's just that I've never seen the two of you kiss."

"Fine," I said, and I kissed her on the cheek.

"No no no," Billy said. "I want to see you kiss her *on the lips*."

*Dammit Billy, you're killing me!*

"Well actually, uh . . . we haven't done that yet," I said.

Billy was dumbfounded and his eyes grew huge like two big moons staring at us.

"You've never kissed on the lips? How long have you two been going out?"

I told him we'd been going out for a month.

"Do you want him to kiss you on the lips?" Billy asked Maria. She nodded her head up and down.

"Yeah," she said. She turned her head and our eyes met. "I do."

"I . . . I can't," I said, looking away. "I'm too nervous." I stood and took a few steps down the street. "Come on, weren't we going to rent a movie?" I led the way to the video store.

If my biggest regret is that I interacted with books more than real people in elementary school, my second biggest regret is that I never kissed Maria, especially when I had such a clear go-ahead. Who gives a shit if Billy was watching? I should have fucking kissed her! Even if it was the worst kiss of my life, at least it would have been *a* kiss! I wouldn't end up kissing a girl until I was nineteen years old and it wasn't even a girl I had any feelings for.

But I'm getting ahead of myself.

Maria broke up with me at the end of the school year via her friend Mallory, who called our house around eleven o'clock in the morning. I was still asleep. My brother woke me up and told me I had a phone call. I stumbled down the stairs and picked up the receiver.

"Hello?"

"Hi Jason. It's Maria's friend. Mallory."

"Hi."

"Hi. Um. I'm sorry to have to tell you this, but . . . Maria wants to break up with you."

"Okay," I said. "Bye."

"Uh . . . bye."

I hung up.

Years later, when my brother broke up with his girlfriend, he referenced this incident when he told me he wished he was as callous with girls as I was.

"It's like you're made of steel when it comes to women," he said. "When that girl in the sixth grade called you and broke up with you, you didn't even flinch. You just said 'okay' and hung up. I wish I could be like that. I get too emotionally invested."

He didn't realize that I *had* been emotionally invested. But I'd seen the breakup coming. What girl wanted a boyfriend too timid to even kiss her? The phone call wasn't a surprise, so I didn't act surprised. But it still hurt to be rejected. It was humiliating to break up with my first girlfriend without ever kissing her. Some part of me was scared I would never have another chance to kiss any girl, ever.

# Aftermath

> Don't part with your illusions. When they are gone you may
> still exist, but you have ceased to live.
> —Mark Twain

After Maria and I broke up, I went back to wallowing around school in loneliness. Thankfully, halfway through the next school year she moved to a different state, so at least I wasn't forced to constantly relive the pain of the breakup every time I passed her in a hallway or we got stuck in the same group for a class project.

Like most of my peers, it was in middle school that I developed a fervent fascination with the female form (which would later transform into a full-blown obsession). My mom had piles of old women's magazines stored in her closet. I'd sneak into it sometimes and find the ones featuring scantily-clad underwear models. I would carefully turn down the corners of the juiciest pages, then sneak them into my bedroom where they would find a resting place beneath my bed.

I'd turn each crisp magazine page slowly and urge myself to find contentment in these two-dimensional beauties. Maria had been a sweet girl, perfect for me, but I'd totally blown it. The unattainable models in my mother's magazines would be my companions from now on.

But to my surprise, another girl caught my eye sooner than I anticipated. Her name was Veronica Keith.

Veronica's waist was slim, but she was curvy in all the right places. She was Filipino, so she had beautifully tanned skin, straight black hair and a cute, flat nose. Her lips were thick and juicy, ripe for kissing.

I first noticed how sexy Veronica was in gym class. The boy's and girl's locker rooms were right across from each other, and as I emerged from the locker room one day I caught sight of Veronica wearing extremely tight, low-cut gym shorts. The derriere that wiggled at me as she walked away was one of the most magnificent sights my thirteen-year-old eyes had ever seen.

Veronica became a recurring character in my late-night fantasies, but that in and of itself was nothing special. Half the girls at our middle school had made regular appearances in my dirty mind each night (sometimes all at the same time). It was only when Veronica started showing me attention that I took a particular interest in her.

Most every crush I've ever had developed in more or less the same way. A girl takes an interest in me by chatting me up now and then and, tantalized by the possibility that she "like likes" me, I become infatuated with her. But because I'm never completely sure whether or not her interest is the result of sexual attraction or whether it's just an effort to make a friend, I'm never able to move beyond friendship. Actually, because my social skills are so poor, I'm not even able to move the relationship *to* friendship—just awkward acquaintanceship.

That's the way it worked with Veronica. One day in gym class after the instructor set us loose to engage in whatever gym activity we wanted, she approached me.

"Hi," she said.

"Hi," I said a little suspiciously. I was always suspicious when girls talked to me. Even though I *wanted* them to talk to me and fall madly in love with me, I always feared they were in cahoots with someone else to embarrass me in front of the entire school.

"How come you're always reading?" she asked.

I shrugged.

"I just like to read."

"What kind of stuff?"

"Science fiction. Robert Heinlein. Arthur C. Clarke. Stuff like that."

"Oh," she said. "Okay."

There was an awkward silence and she walked away.

It seemed like flirting to me. Inept flirting, but flirting nonetheless. Why would she talk to me if she wasn't at least a little interested, even if the questions themselves weren't particularly flirtatious? Maybe she just took pity on my loneliness.

Even if she *was* trying to flirt with me, I was too terrified to flirt back. To my conspiratorial mind, that's exactly what the popular kids wanted me to do. They'd see me show an interest in this hottie and proclaim, "Look at Jason! He thinks he has a chance with Veronica Keith—what a loser!"

But Veronica kept talking to me every now and then. It was just often enough to keep me infatuated. She expertly strung me along, whether she realized it or not. Whenever my hopes began to fade and I decided I'd only imagined her attraction to me, she approached me and my hopes flew sky-high again.

Recently, some friends and I were discussing at what point we and our classmates first became sexually aware. When I claimed it was in middle school, they scoffed. Yeah, they said, middle school kids can be sexual, but it's a naïve, ignorant sexuality. They don't really know what they're talking about. I argued that at *my* middle school, at least, almost every student was obsessed with sex and they knew, more or less, what they were talking about. Perhaps my own hypersexuality skewed my memories, but I would bet money that we were all a bunch of horny little freaks.

Either way, sex was always a hot topic of discussion at my middle school, and for some reason, many kids started using the term "monkey butt sex" as if it were a common slang phrase. I don't know if this was a term circulating throughout middle schools across the country or if it was isolated to our rural school, but I heard it surprisingly frequently.

One day I overheard two girls talking about who wanted to have "monkey butt sex" with whom. They were going through nearly everyone in the school, typical girly gossip, although the brazen sexuality of their conversation still managed to take me aback. The subsequent turn the conversation took *really* took me by surprise.

"Veronica wants to have monkey butt sex with who? *Cole*?"

Veronica Keith, the girl I pined after, that I fantasized about countless nights, wanted to have monkey butt sex with *me*?

Just then, Veronica walked by and the girls called out to her.

"You want to have monkey butt sex with Jason Cole?"

She didn't acknowledge them. She kept walking straight to class. I didn't know what to make of that. Did she ignore them because their conclusion was true and she was embarrassed or because it wasn't . . . and she was even more embarrassed? I couldn't tell. I don't think it even mattered. If she'd turned around and said, "Yes, it's true, I want to have the dirtiest, nastiest monkey butt sex imaginable with Jason Cole, all night, every night for as long as we're both alive," I think I would have fled. As a virgin, how could I not be intimidated by such a declaration?

But she didn't say that and our awkward acquaintanceship remained an awkward acquaintanceship.

Middle school marked the end of an awkward chapter in my life, but I didn't know an even more awkward chapter lay ahead. I lived far away from my middle school. My parents thought it would help me to go to a bigger middle school (because even though the one I went to was small, the one in my hometown was even smaller). But now I would go to high school in my hometown. I would leave behind everyone I knew in middle school. I was certain I would never see Veronica Keith again. I concluded that all the awkward flirting (if it could be called flirting) had been in vain. Maybe high school would be better, but I wasn't sure. Once again, I was entering a brave new world in which I didn't know a soul.

# High School

Reality is merely an illusion, albeit a very persistent one.
—Albert Einstein

I PRAYED HIGH SCHOOL WOULD BE BETTER THAN MIDDLE school.

I decided to make the biggest effort of my life to build real, strong, healthy relationships with people. My four years in high school were supposed to be the best years of my life. At least, that's what TV shows and movies always told me. If I didn't leave high school with great memories, and great friends, I could consider my life a failure.

My mom took me clothes shopping a couple weeks before school started. In middle school the kids wore baggy clothes and I took the trend a bit too far, buying clothes that were not just baggy, but woefully oversized. I never had very good fashion sense.

That didn't change in high school. I tried to imitate the styles I saw, but not with much success. Of course, I didn't realize that at the time; I thought I looked pretty cool. Gradually, as I studied the clothes of the people around me, I realized I didn't look nearly as cool as I thought, but I was helpless. My sense of fashion was nonexistent and I was too shy to ask anyone for help picking out clothes.

Besides, I didn't plan to make friends through my style. I figured my first English class would be my chance to shine. For some reason, I always thought my writing ability would impress guys and girls alike. Guys would want to be my friend and girls would be desperate to make love to me.

I pictured my English teacher, Mr. Powell, getting up in front of class with an essay I'd written, telling all the other students, "*This* is how you write an essay. *This* is how you convey information through the written word. You would all be well served to learn from Mr. Cole." All the guys in the class would turn to look at me and nod their heads in respect. All the girls would turn to stare at me reverently, undressing me with their eyes.

Not only was I grossly overestimating my writing ability, I was also neglecting the fact that nobody in high school really gives a shit about academics—not in determining popularity, anyway. They might care if you write something particularly funny, but otherwise all they care about is sports. If you can run quickly or throw a mean fastball or tackle a 300-pound behemoth, then you might gain some respect. But write a short story you think is cool, or an essay that gets accolades from the English teacher, and the most one can hope for is shrugs, if not outright scorn.

I wasn't an athlete. Far from it. In elementary school I joined a junior baseball league, so I could hold my own at baseball, but I didn't excel at it. I could hit grounders and catch a pop-fly, but I threw like a girl. I barely knew how to play basketball and I didn't know *any* of football's rules.

If writing wasn't cool, and sports were beyond my ability, I figured I had to find some other way to fit in and make friends. I joined the school band (I played the trumpet), attended football and basketball games (as a spectator only, of course), and joined a marketing club. I had fun, but I still wasn't able to make any real close friends.

I made my first real high school friend at my church's youth group.

Nathan Everett was tall and large. He was somewhat overweight, but would have been large regardless—he's what people call "big boned."

Bonding over humor sparked a friendship with Billy in middle school. Once again, humor served as the common element that united Nathan and me in friendship.

His sense of humor ranged from dry to sarcastic. It was scathing and he didn't spare anyone (including me).

A genuine faith in God burned within Nathan, but he also felt social pressure to fit the "class clown" mold. He set aside his jokes in favor of more serious conversation at times, but it was rare. I didn't care. He made me laugh.

Nathan's dad was a teacher at a nearby high school (not ours, which I'm sure he appreciated) and when Nathan decided to go on a weekend retreat, his dad told him to look out for one of his students who would also be going. Her name was Riley Williams.

Blogs were just becoming popular when I was in high school and nearly everyone at our school used the blogging website LiveJournal. This was well before MySpace or Facebook became popular, so LiveJournal doubled as both a blogging platform and a social network.

One day I noticed a new user commenting on Nathan's posts. They were funny, and I asked Nathan who it was.

"It's that girl Riley, the one I met at the retreat."

"Oh," I said. "Are you guys . . . you know . . ."

"No! Not at all. We're just friends."

"Do you mind if I talk to her?"

"Go ahead. What do I care?"

I sent her a message. We began instant messaging each other regularly. She had a sharp sense of humor, almost identical to Nathan's, and I could see why they had hit it off so quickly. I enjoyed talking to her. I joked that, since I had never met her to confirm her existence, she was probably just Nathan pretending to be someone else as a prank. She shot the same accusation right back at me.

I didn't realize it yet, but Nathan and Riley would become two of my best friends in the world. They remain so to this day.

RILEY AND I both liked the band Switchfoot, so I invited her to go to a music festival they were headlining.

"Sure," she said.

First, I had to get permission from my parents to go—a ritual that always left me stung from embarrassment. It always took a supreme effort to get my overprotective parents to relinquish even the tiniest bit of control over my life.

"Mom, Dad," I said. "Is it okay if I go to a concert with someone?"

"With who?" Mom asked.

"My friend Riley."

Both their eyebrows perked up in interest.

"Is this a *girl*friend?" Dad asked. The emphasis on the world

## High School

"girl" made the sexual undertones clear.

"No," I said quickly. "Definitely not. She's a friend of Nathan's. They met at that retreat he went to."

"How old is she?" Mom asked suspiciously.

"Sixteen," I said. "A year younger than me."

"I'm not sure I want you hanging out with a girl that young... She probably doesn't have much experience driving. If you get in her car and drive somewhere, who knows what could happen..."

*Good lord*, I thought. *Here we go again.* Why couldn't my parents let me be a teenager? Millions of teens across the country were allowed to hang out with their friends without so much as a goodbye to their parents, and here were mine giving me the third degree over *one* concert.

"Mom, I'm a junior in high school. I have my driver's license. I'm going to be a legal adult in a year. Can you guys please just trust me enough to go to this one stupid concert?"

My parents turned toward each other and exchanged a look.

"Give us a minute to talk privately," Mom said.

I left the room and after a couple minutes they called me back in.

"You can go," she said, and a thrill shot through me. "But we have some ground rules. I want you to write down this girl's name, address and cell phone number, and her mom's number... just in case something happens."

Getting Riley's mom's phone number would be completely mortifying, but I was so excited for the concert I was willing to do pretty much anything.

"And have your cell phone on the whole time," Dad added.

"Yeah," I said eagerly. "That's fine."

"One more thing," Mom said as I turned to go. "You have to take your brother with you."

I stopped and turned around. "But Mom—"

"Fine, if you don't want to go—"

"No, no," I said quickly. "That's okay. He can come."

The day of the concert was one of the hottest days of the summer, reaching triple digits, which was fairly unusual for western Oregon.

"Who's playing?" my brother, Tim, asked on the way to the concert.

"Switchfoot."

"Who?"

"Don't worry," I said. "You'll like them."

Parking cost ten dollars and consisted of a huge dirt field lined with cars. It took us fifteen minutes, driving up and down, to find a space. We had to jam our car in so tight we could barely squeeze through the doors.

"Okay," I said. "Time to find Riley."

I pulled out our cell phone (my parents had just recently put a third phone on their plan and forced my brother and I to share it) and dialed Riley's number.

After a few rounds of phone tag, we met up in the parking lot.

Riley's hair was a bright, fiery red. Her skin, nearly as pale as a ghost, only made the color of her hair stand out more.

She brought a friend with her whose name was also Tim, just like my brother. We had a laugh about that, then walked into the main concert grounds.

We watched one of the bands on the fringe stage for a while, but Riley wasn't into it.

"It's too hot," she said. "Tim and I are going to go wait in the car and crank up the AC."

The thought of Riley and Tim sitting alone together in her car sent waves of jealousy through me.

I hadn't really realized it until that point, but I'd enjoyed bantering back and forth with her so much I'd developed a crush on her.

"Don't you want to see the bands?" I asked.

"I just came for Switchfoot. Come on, Tim. Let's go."

"Later," I said unenthusiastically.

My brother and I sat side by side, arms folded across our chest, watching the band.

"These guys suck," he said.

"Whatever," I replied. I wasn't listening to the band. My mind was with Riley and Tim sitting in her car.

Were they in there joking and laughing? Gossiping? Making out? I couldn't help thinking it could be *me* in there making out with her if I were only a little more bold and confident.

The sun set and it grew cooler. Riley and Tim exited her vehicle like bears emerging from their cave after a long hibernation.

"We didn't miss Switchfoot yet, did we?" Riley asked.

"No, but they're next," I said. "Good timing."

We laid a blanket on the grass and sat down during the soundcheck, waiting for the band we had come to see.

The show was electrifying. They played a lot of music from a new album none of us had ever heard, so it was difficult to sing along to many of the songs. But they still played several fan favorites, and we were afforded ample opportunity to strain our vocal chords.

I was tired when we parted ways at the end of the night, but I knew that despite my confused feelings about her, Riley would be a good friend for a long time.

## Summer of Salvia

Nathan, Riley and I all lived far away from each other, so we didn't hang out every day that summer. I would have loved to—they were my closest friends—but the infrequent outings we had together were fun times for me nonetheless.

One night the three of us went to a drive-in movie theater in Newberg with a few mutual friends. The movie, *The Day After Tomorrow*, was memorably bad. But it wasn't the movie I remember from that night.

All three of us shared a similar sense of humor, but Riley and Nathan seemed to take to each other and I felt left out. Worse, they seemed to be flirting with each other and I watched them laugh at each other's jokes through envious eyes.

The next day, I spoke with Riley on the phone. She had something to confess, she said.

"I have a crush on Nathan!"

My heart deflated instantly. "That's, um . . . that's great."

I was crushed, but I didn't want my disappointment to be apparent. I couldn't let on that this news disturbed me. If I did, my crush on Riley would be out in the open—a thought I couldn't tolerate.

Over time, my feelings for Riley became completely platonic. She is probably my best friend as I'm writing this. I share more with her than with anyone, save my immediate family. Even then, there's much I don't share. I'm a very private person. Maybe that's unhealthy, maybe not. But I do know that when I feel like I need to talk to someone, Riley is almost always there. It's a great comfort to me and I wouldn't trade that friendship for anything.

# Community College

> You are an aperture through which the universe
> is looking at and exploring itself.
> —Alan W. Watts

Community college.
Just saying it leaves a dirty taste in one's mouth, but the bum rap community colleges get is largely undeserved.

My family is middle class. Not lower-middle class, not upper-middle class—middle-middle class. I didn't expect my family to pay for my entire college education. Thus, in the spirit of fiscal responsibility and frugality, I spent my first two years out of high school at a community college.

But attending a community college wasn't my only rite of passage. I also had to find a job.

I applied to a variety of fast food and retail locations—what some people call "McJobs"—and nobody called me back for an interview. Worry set in. I'd never had a part-time job in high school. I'd wanted one, but I'd lived so far out in the sticks that walking or public transportation weren't options. I needed a car and the only way I could get a car was with money. The only way I could make money was by getting a job. And the only way I could get to a job was if I had a car.

Basically, I was screwed.

Consequently, I had zero job experience on my applications. It would be an uphill battle for that reason, but I didn't realize it would be difficult to find even a fast food job.

Finally, I got a break. Elaine, an older lady at our church, had a daughter that worked in the human resources department at a FedEx hub. They had an entry-level opening for a package handler. It was October and they were preparing for the incredible shitstorm about to rain down upon them known as the "holiday season." Elaine said she would put in a good word for me.

I wore a pair of khaki pants and a white button-down shirt to the interview. I didn't have a tie. I hoped I looked professional enough.

I walked in and asked for Katherine—Elaine's daughter. She came down a stairway in the corner and greeted me.

"Hi Jason, I'm Katherine." She held out her hand and I shook it.

"Nice to meet you," I said cheerfully.

"Come on up," she said and walked back up the stairs she'd just walked down. I followed obediently.

She ushered me into her office, sat down and brought my application up on her computer. She asked a couple of questions about school activities and other stuff that didn't seem all that relevant to me. Then the questions got nerve-racking.

"Do you exercise regularly?" she asked.

"Um . . . well, I've been trying to exercise more often, yeah."

"How often?"

"I usually run for about a half hour. About three times a week."

"The reason I ask is that this job is physically demanding. I want to make sure you feel that's something you can handle."

*Dear lord, what am I getting myself into?*

"Of course," I said. "I'm sure I can handle it." I needed this job, even if I had to lie to get it.

"Good. Can you drive a stick?"

Could I drive a stick? I thought I was going to be throwing boxes around, not delivering them.

"Uh . . . no, actually."

"Oh. Well, that's going to be a problem . . ."

"I didn't know I needed to—"

"Part of the job involves washing the trucks and you have to move them around to the front parking lot to wash them. Most of the trucks are stick shifts."

"I'm sure I can learn quickly."

"Can you learn how to drive a stick in a week, before you start?"

*Hell no!*

"Yes," I said. "Of course. I'll get my parents to teach me."

She paused and scrunched her lips tight as if weighing whether I meant what I said, whether I was worth the risk of hiring. I waited there, sweating, the suspense killing me.

"Well . . . Okay. You're hired."

I wasn't sure whether to be happy or scared shitless.

Around the same time I landed my new job at FedEx, I made a friend online. Her name was Katie and while I was somewhat sexually attracted to her, it was clear we were better suited as friends than lovers. It wasn't the kind of situation where the guy secretly pines after the girl, but is obliviously relegated to the "friend zone." I genuinely enjoyed hanging out with her as a friend with no sexual tension eating away at the fun.

While Katie was a devout Christian, something I admired and respected about her, she wasn't without her vices. She was prone to self-medication. Drinking was nothing new to her, but shortly after I started hanging out with her, she began smoking marijuana frequently.

I often argued with her about it, telling her she shouldn't be getting high, that it wasn't good to be in an altered state of mind like that. She adamantly disagreed.

One night, a thought occurred to me. How could I effectively argue against something I had never tried myself? Wasn't it a bit hypocritical? Katie's central argument, that pot was safe compared to alcohol, made some sense. Shouldn't I at least try it once? As the saying goes, "Don't knock it 'til you've tried it."

I sent Katie a text message: I WANT YOU TO GET ME HIGH.

Her reply was prompt: YES! OMG, I'M SO EXCITED! COME OVER TONIGHT. I'LL GET YOU SO BAKED!

She was house-sitting for her boss, so when I came over she directed me to the back porch.

"We can't smoke in here," she said. "Otherwise it'll smell like pot smoke when Cassandra gets back, and I will be in deep, deep shit."

"Not a problem," I said.

We sat down on lawn chairs and she removed a small glass pipe, a lighter, and a baggie of marijuana from her sweatshirt pockets. She pinched a marijuana bud between her fingers and dropped it into the bowl.

## Community College

"It can be a little tricky your first time, but here's how it works," she said. "You grab the pipe and cover up this little hole here with your thumb." She pointed to a little opening on the side of the bowl of the pipe. "While you're doing that, you put the end in your mouth and start inhaling. Then, you take the lighter and light the weed in the bowl. You release the hole, and you inhale all the smoke into your lungs. You hold it in for as long as you can, and then you exhale. The longer you hold in the smoke, the higher you get."

"Okay. I'm ready to try."

I was nervous. I had never done drugs before. I'd never intended to. I was crossing a line by doing this. I knew once it was crossed there was no going back.

I had trouble lighting the bowl while also covering the hole and sucking in the smoke. My first couple tries were unsuccessful and finally, in frustration, Katie grabbed the lighter and lit the bowl for me.

I held in the smoke, and after only a few seconds began coughing uncontrollably.

"Oh man," Katie laughed, "you're going to get so high!"

"I don't feel any different."

"You will."

She lit a bowl for herself, then lit it for me again. After a few more turns back and forth, she decided the bowl was pretty much spent and we went inside.

Katie's boss had a nice pool table, so we agreed to play a couple games. I still wasn't feeling any different. Shortly after the first break, it struck me.

When I moved my eyes, it seemed to take a few seconds for the images to catch up. My eyes wouldn't focus and it was like everything moved in slow motion.

After a minute, it didn't just *look* like things were moving in slow motion. I felt like *I* was moving in slow motion.

Needless to say, this did not improve my pool game.

"Okay," I said. "It's starting to hit me."

"Isn't it incredible? I feel awesome!"

"It's weird," I said. "It's kind of cool, I guess."

"What's it like for you?"

"It's like everything's in slow motion."

"I totally get what you mean."

"My eyes are, like . . . it's like I can feel them rolling around in their sockets."

Katie grabbed her pool cue and prepared to take a shot, then stopped and looked up at me quizzically.

"Whose shot is it?" she asked.

"I . . . I have no idea. I forgot we were even playing pool. Hey! I'm going to put on some music."

I had recently discovered Jack Johnson, and Katie had never heard his music, so I brought one of his CDs with me.

We went through a couple songs as we played. Suddenly, Katie decided to make her opinion of the soft, soothing acoustic music very clear.

"This is boring," she whined.

"It is not boring!" I was completely aghast. My newfound love for Jack Johnson ran deep, and Katie telling me he was boring was like her telling me my mom was a whore.

"I respect that you like him," Katie said diplomatically, "But I'm going to put on some of my music now."

She popped in a Black-Eyed Peas CD and subjected me to some of the worst music I'd ever heard.

"Jack Johnson may be boring," I said, "But at least he's not retarded, like these guys are."

"They are *not* retarded! Here, listen to this song. The lyrics are amazing. They're really deep."

She switched the track and played the song "Gone Going."

I listened to the song thinking to myself, 'Okay, these lyrics are a little deeper than the rest of the Black-Eyed Peas songs Katie's made me listen to tonight.' But then the chorus started.

"Katie!" I shouted. "That's Jack Johnson!"

"No it isn't. It's the Black-Eyed Peas."

"The guy singing the chorus—that's Jack Johnson."

"No it isn't."

"I'd know that voice anywhere! That is Jack Johnson!"

"Prove it."

"Where's the CD case?"

She handed it to me and I pulled out the liner notes. I scanned through them, found the lyrics for the song "Gone Going," and pointed triumphantly.

"Right there," I said. "'Lyrics by Jack Johnson.'"

I laughed manically. Katie slapped me on the shoulder.

"Quit laughing at me!"

"I can't help it," I said between laughs. "I think it's the pot!"

I slept at Katie's house that night (well, Katie's boss's house) and woke up on the couch, still a bit high. I cursed. I had class, and I didn't have enough time to go home and take a shower and change. I would have to go to class reeking of marijuana.

I walked out the door without waking Katie, determined to never smoke marijuana again.


I HAVE NEVER been more exhausted than after my first week at FedEx.

My muscles ached more than anything on my body had ever

ached before. Muscles I didn't know I had ached. It wasn't just my arms. Every inch of my body was sore.

Every night, for most of my shift, I was stuck in the back of a freight truck. The packages rolled down a conveyer belt. Someone collected them, scanned them, and threw them into the trailer, where I waited to grab and stack them, constructing a solid wall of packages. It was a lot like *Tetris*, except I couldn't sit on the couch and eat potato chips while I did it.

At first it was easy enough. The packages rolled in at a moderate pace.

Then they streamed in.

And then they *flooded* in.

They came in faster than I could stack them. I'm not talking about teeny tiny packages. Some of these boxes were *huge!* I barely made it through that first week alive.

A week before I started work, I'd asked Bob, a guy from our church in his early fifties who drove an old Mitsubishi pick-up, if he could teach me how to drive a stick shift. He agreed . . . perhaps against his better judgment.

By the end of the day, I could drive a stick shift . . . but just barely. In the process, I'd heard Bob utter more swear words than I would have thought he knew.

Unfortunately, driving a huge delivery truck was a little different than driving Bob's little pick-up. I could barely maneuver the truck to the front of the building to be washed.

How was I going to get through a month of this?

It wasn't just my muscles and my driving skills that were uncomfortable. My coworkers' favorite topic of discussion during downtime soon became apparent: sex.

Nearly every word out their mouths was about banging some chick they'd seen in a magazine or what it would be like to bed

## COMMUNITY COLLEGE

some celebrity.

Sean was the worst of them.

He was twenty-two, three years older than me, but he looked young—at first I thought he was around eighteen, like me. He had dark skin, and I never did find out what his ethnicity was. He looked Hispanic to me.

The kid had raging hormones that put mine to shame. Literally every word out of his mouth chronicled his efforts to get laid. He constantly lamented his virginity. I didn't mention that I, myself, had never known a woman, although I suppose it was obvious. In fact, I didn't participate in any of the dirty conversations my coworkers had. I just listened, which is probably why I didn't make any particularly close friends during my stint at FedEx.

Although I may not have been as vocal about my libido as Sean was, every night when I got off work I'd run into my house, get on the internet, and scope out chicks. I told myself I only used these dating sites to find a girlfriend, someone I could get into a Godly, long-term, abstinent relationship with. But deep down I knew I just wanted to get laid, exactly like ninety-nine percent of the other douchebag guys on those websites. But I had very little luck getting any of these girls to meet me for a date, let alone a hook-up.

Now and then I picked up a copy of the local alternative weekly newspaper. It was free and interesting; it killed the time as I waited for work to start after class.

The back of the newspaper was plastered with ads for prostitutes. I always told myself to ignore that part of the paper. I pleaded with myself to just set it down before temptation got the best of me. Sometimes it worked. But usually I gave in. I'd flip to the back of the paper. My eyes would drink in the sight of scantily clad beauties painted in smeared ink onto crisp newsprint.

## Summer of Salvia

In my mind, I removed what little clothing they wore in their photos and imagined my hands roaming over their flesh, our lips touching, our tongues winding around each other.

Then I would lock myself in a bathroom and masturbate furiously. I always felt extravagantly guilty afterward. It was like my innocence was draining away, perched in the bowels of a crumpled-up tissue, sucked up by the hungry mouth of the toilet bowl.

I'd never seriously considered seeing one of these prostitutes, for a variety of obvious reasons. One was the risk of contracting a venereal disease. Second was the risk of getting caught in a sting operation. I could picture myself calling my parents from jail, telling them I'd been arrested for soliciting a prostitute. Third was the fact that I simply couldn't afford one.

But I was desperate for sex. And when I'd saved up enough money from my job at FedEx, I finally caved. I picked up the weekly paper, found the ad for the cheapest prostitute I could find, and dialed.

# Debauchery

> A wise man, recognizing the world is but an illusion, does not act as if it were real, so he escapes the suffering.
> —Buddha

With each ring of the phone, my heart beat a little faster, my breath grew a little shorter. *Holy crap. Am I really doing this? Am I really calling a fucking hooker?* Some part of me was horrified by the notion. Another part was exhilarated.

"Hello?" a disinterested voice said.

"Uh ... hi. Is this, uh ... Holly?"

"Yes it is."

"Hi. Uh. I'm calling about your ad in the *Mercury*."

"Okay."

"So. Um. I've never really done this before ..."

"Would you like to schedule an appointment?"

"Yeah."

"When?"

"Um. Well. In about an hour, if possible. At seven."

"Okay. Did you want to pay for an hour session, or a half hour?"

"Half hour." I couldn't imagine I'd last a whole hour. Hell, ten minutes would probably be more than enough time.

"Alright."

She gave me general directions to her apartment. "When you get that far, call me and I'll tell you how to get the rest of the way," she said. Why she couldn't give me the full directions to begin with, I had no idea, but I chocked it up to hooker etiquette and told her it was fine.

It occurred to me I'd have to pay in cash, so I drove to a gas station to use their ATM. Just as I pulled into the parking lot, my phone rang and the caller ID said it was from an unidentified number. I answered. It was Holly.

"I'm not going to be able to keep our appointment," she said. "My next-door neighbor usually watches my kids when I'm with . . . clients . . . and she's sick. But I work with a couple other girls, and I'd be willing to set you up with one of them for seven-thirty if that's okay with you."

"Um . . . yeah," I said, a little annoyed but nowhere near assertive enough to complain.

"There's a couple different girls. Catherine is blonde like me. She's really cute, has a nice chest. I think you'd like her a lot. Then there's Jasmine. She's Puerto Rican and has dark, chocolaty skin. Her ass is killer."

I thought it over a moment, but not for long. I couldn't resist the tantalizing allure of a nice ass.

"I'll go with Jasmine," I said.

"Let me give her a call. Go ahead and make like you're coming to my place; she doesn't live too far from me. I'll call you back when I have everything set up."

I got some cash from the ATM and continued on my way. After a few minutes Holly called and told me I had the green light with Jasmine.

When I was in the general vicinity I called Holly back and got the final directions to Jasmine's apartment, as well as the apartment number: Eight.

The apartment complex was two stories tall and four units wide. The paint was peeling and coated in dirt. A variety of beat-up cars lined the parking lot. It was a seedy little joint—it looked like the setting of the conclusion of a manhunt, when the cops corner a bank robber or a serial killer in a little rat-hole motel room and the whole thing ends in a bloody shootout. Suddenly I was nervous not only because I was about to lose my virginity to a whore, but also because I might get robbed or even killed here, *without* ever getting my dick wet. I might die a virgin.

I walked up the stairs to the upper level, watching my feet to make sure the rotting steps didn't buckle under my weight and send me tumbling to the hospital with a broken leg. When I cleared the stairs, I walked to apartment eight and knocked on the door.

I heard someone unlock the deadbolt. The door creaked open slowly to reveal a dark-skinned woman that looked like she was in her late twenties.

I gave a sigh of relief. Since I hadn't seen a picture of this girl, I'd feared she might be hideous. But she was hot. She had a cute face, framed by silky black hair that came down to her armpits. Her waist was narrow and she had long legs. While she didn't have boobs that would've made Dolly Parton jealous, she was far from flat-chested.

"Jason?" I nodded. "Come on in," she said.

I entered slowly, taking in the place. It looked like a normal apartment. Certainly nothing fancy, but not a total dump, either. The carpeting was clean, there was a nice little entertainment center set up, and the furniture was all in good condition. The interior was certainly more hospitable than the exterior.

"You a cop?" she asked.

I was surprised by how casually she asked the question.

"No," I stuttered out. I was nervous, but I was prepared for that question—I'd looked up hooker etiquette online and several sites mentioned it was common for them to ask that question to make sure they weren't getting embroiled in a sting operation. I was supposed to ask the same question, to make sure *I* wasn't being set up by a cop, but I was too intimidated by her. *Fuck it*, I thought.

"You have the money?"

"Yep. Right here." I pulled the wad of cash out of my pocket and handed it to her. She counted it, then looked up and nodded at me.

"Go ahead and take off your clothes," she said. "I'll be right back." She walked into the other room. As she walked away I checked out her ass. It looked as good as advertised.

"Here we go," I said to myself, and as quickly as I could, I pulled off all my clothes.

She came back into the room, naked, and sat down on the couch.

"Come sit down," she said, patting the empty couch space beside her. I sat down next to her.

She grabbed a bottle of moisturizing lotion and squirted some into her hands.

## Debauchery

"Do you have more money?" she asked. "For tips?"

*Tips? Are you a whore or a waitress?*

"I . . . uh . . . no. I didn't know I was supposed to. I've never done this before."

"For future reference, this is how it works: In addition to the ninety-dollar fee, you pay tips for any additional services you want. So, a handjob would be twenty dollars, a blowjob would be forty dollars, intercourse would be seventy-five dollars. Okay?"

"Oh. Okay," I said, trying not to let my disappointment come through in my voice.

"So I'll just go ahead and give you a hand job," she said. She placed her lotion-coated hands onto my penis.

It felt odd, having a woman stroke my penis. It wasn't at all like I thought it would be. I mean, I stroked my penis just about every night and it felt great. Now that this hooker was stroking my cock, it should have felt incredible.

It didn't.

She wasn't so much caressing my penis as manhandling it. She whipped her hands up and down roughly, and, despite the lotion's lubrication, it *hurt*. Not a lot, but enough to make this a much more uncomfortable experience than I'd hoped it would be. But I was too timid to say anything, and the excitement of having a woman's hands on my penis, no matter how much discomfort it brought me, was enough to maintain my erection. *Great*, I thought, *I'm not even going to get laid, I'm just going to get the worst hand job ever. This sucks.*

"You can touch me," Jasmine said and she spread her legs.

"Oh," I said. I brought my hand to her vagina and gently cupped it. It was warm. "Oh, wow," I said.

"Don't just touch it like it's an armrest or something," she said. "Caress it."

"I'm sorry. I just . . . I've never done any of this before . . ."

"Wait." Her hands stopped. "You've never had *sex*? You're a *virgin*?"

"Well . . . yeah."

She immediately got up. *Oh man, what did I do? Is she getting a gun?*

"I can't believe you're a virgin!" she yelled. She walked into the other room and when she walked back in she was unwrapping a condom.

She sat back down beside me, slipped the rubber onto my penis and then, as I was sitting there, dumbfounded, she straddled me.

"There you go," she said through her teeth as she lowered herself onto my manhood. "There's a pussy for you." I couldn't believe this was happening. A minute ago it had seemed I wasn't getting laid; now all of a sudden, there was a woman straddling me. It was all happening too quickly. My breath came out in frantic gasps.

"Here," she said, lifting my hands and putting them on her hips. "Feel my body. Feel that *ass*."

I did. I cupped her ass cheeks and they felt wonderful. Her body was so warm and lovely, but . . . my penis couldn't feel a fucking thing. *Is this it? Is this what all the hype is about?*

"Don't just lie there," she said. "Move your hips up and down." I did. Or tried to, anyway. My legs weren't that strong, and it was difficult to thrust upward with the weight of her body on top of me.

"You haven't had pussy," she said. "But have you sucked on titties?" She thrust her right tit into my face, and I didn't bother to answer her question. I sucked her nipple into my mouth eagerly. I hadn't sucked on a woman's breast since I'd been breastfed.

## Debauchery

Suddenly, even though my dick was numb, a tingling sensation crept over my body. Every inch of my skin prickled. It was almost like numbness, but more intense, and in a way it was almost the opposite of numbness—my skin was ultra-sensitive. I moaned into Jasmine's neck.

"Did you come yet?" she asked.

"I . . . don't know . . ."

She continued for a few moments and then asked again if I'd come. It annoyed me a little. Hadn't I paid for a half hour? It had only been fifteen minutes.

When I said I didn't know if I'd come, I really didn't know. The only sensation I had was this intense tingling, and it didn't extend to my penis; I couldn't feel anything down there. But she sounded eager to end.

"Yeah," I said. "I think I did."

She pulled herself off me and I gently pulled off the condom. I cupped it in my hand so she couldn't see it, because I wasn't sure if I had come or not, and I didn't want her to feel embarrassed if I hadn't. My blood still pounded through my veins, but the tingling sensation gradually diminished.

"Well," she said as I sat there recovering, "You ain't a virgin no more."

As I got dressed, she asked the one question I didn't want to answer.

"Why have you never had sex?" she asked. "You're not bad lookin'."

"I don't know," I said. "I just get nervous around girls, so I've never really had the opportunity to."

"Hmm." She thought a moment. "You should ask girls out," she said. "Just go to the mall or something. Girls love to be asked out. And when you take her out, make her a nice meal and get her a bottle of wine—that'll get you both calm and relaxed. And then . . . you can just take it from there."

"Yeah," I said. "I guess." *Like it's that easy. And I can't even buy wine yet.*

"And if you feel like you need someone to teach you more about sex, so you feel more experienced," she said as I headed out the door, "you just give me a call."

I drove directly from her apartment into a McDonald's parking lot. I had to take a piss and after losing my virginity to a hooker and all, I was a little hungry. I got a hamburger and water to go, and as I sat in my car eating, I replayed again and again what had just happened. And although I felt a little dirty and sleazy, and I was praying for God to forgive me, I couldn't wipe the grin off my face.

For me, horniness and guilt come in peaks and troughs, like a roller coaster. For a little while—it could be a few weeks, it could be a couple months—I'll be at the top of a wave of horniness, while the guilt that keeps me from acting on my primal urges is stuck in a trough below. Then I'll go through a phase where thinking even the slightest impure thought fills me with unimaginable guilt, and it's the sexual urges stuck in the gully below.

Usually one phase sets off the other. So if I've been on a horn-dog streak, masturbating five times a day to the nastiest pornography I can scrounge up online for free, eventually I'll feel so dirty and depraved that I'll go into guilt-ridden Christian schoolboy mode. On the other end of the spectrum, when I've been in my (relatively) pure mode awhile, it seems like the underlying debauchery within me builds and builds and builds until it's bubbling out of me and finally I act out sexually. It's a

## Debauchery

never-ending cycle.* Like life, I guess.

Often, when in sinful mode, I would log into dating websites looking for sex partners. It always proved fruitless, but I was determined to find a girl to have sex with. After having sex with a hooker, I was desperate to find a girl who would have sex with me because she wanted to—and for *free*.

I'd been chatting with a girl named Melissa on a dating site awhile, just off and on. I wasn't getting my hopes up with her for a couple reasons. She lived an hour and a half away, and while I was definitely willing to travel that far for some nookie, my efforts were focused on girls closer to me. Secondly, she wasn't ugly, but she wasn't a knockout, either.

We instant messaged back and forth and when I broached the possibility of meeting each other, she surprised me by enthusiastically agreeing that we should meet.

Okay, I told her. Let's go to the drive-in.

Ooooh, she typed back. You know what happens at drive-ins ;)

No. What?

Nothing good ;) ;) ;)

Hmm. Maybe you should skip wearing panties altogether then.

Maybe I will.

Now I had an erection and a racing heart.

I drove for an hour and a half to pick her up. She was dressed to the nines, but I was slightly disappointed with how chubby she was—she'd looked slimmer in her photos. But I scolded myself. *Come on, Jason. You're being a shallow asshole. Get to know*

---

* In hindsight, it's a cycle of addiction—sex addiction. I didn't even realize I was a sex addict when I started this book, but now, years later, I can't believe I didn't realize it sooner.

*this girl a little!*

We teased each other on the way to the drive-in. I'd been working on my flirting skills, and I was confident it was my hard work that had finally landed me this success. In hindsight, I think it's more probable that Melissa was merely as desperate as I was to get laid.

When we pulled into the theater and parked, we sat there for a long while, waiting for the movie to come onto the screen. After it started, we mostly watched in silence, although now and then we made comments to each other.

After a while, she turned to me and said, "Are you ticklish?"

"No," I said.

"Are you sure?" There was a devilish gleam in her eye and I didn't like where this was going.

"Yeah. I'm sure."

"Let's find out!" Suddenly her hands roamed over my body, not sensually, but in jagged pokes and prods. She tickled me like somebody might tickle their four-year-old niece.

And I was *laughing* like someone's four-year-old niece.

"Stop, stop it!" I cried through my tears. She didn't let up so I decided to launch a counterassault. My hands shot toward her armpits and she burst into laughter.

"How do you like it?" I said excitedly. Suddenly we were embroiled in a tickle war of epic proportions.

It would have been romantic if the tickles had transformed into gentle caresses and we'd ended up staring longingly into each other's eyes. If I'd then leaned over and kissed her softly on the lips, then kissed her again, my lips lingering just a bit longer, until, before I knew what was happening, my mouth was enveloping hers, hungrily feasting upon the warmth of her breath as it met mine and congealed, becoming the breath of a single, unified being.

# DEBAUCHERY

In reality, we stopped tickling each other and awkwardly went back to watching the movie. But clearly she didn't have the movie on her mind.

"Do you want to kiss me?" she asked.

*Sister, I want to do a lot more than just kiss you.*

"Yes," I said. "But, uh . . . I've never kissed a girl before."

It was true. Here I was, nineteen years old, and I had still never kissed a girl. I'd had sex with a hooker (*sans* kissing), but I had not so much as pecked a girl on the lips.

She was surprised, but not as shocked as I'd expected. Clearly she wanted me to kiss her and felt insecure that I hadn't. I'm sure she thought it was because I wasn't attracted to her. But what I told her gave her renewed self-confidence. She understood now that it wasn't that I found her unattractive. I was just inexperienced. I was nervous and shy. Suddenly our roles reversed; *she* became the bold, daring, take-action male, as I transformed into the timid, shy, submissive female.

"You've never kissed a girl before? Well let's change that," she said with a grin. She leaned over and kissed me.

Just as sex was in some ways not at all as wonderful as I'd expected, kissing was not the mind-blowing, transcendent experience I had built up in my head. It was an underwhelming experience that left me disappointed. I'm not exactly sure what I'd been expecting, but the experience was much more pedestrian than I had anticipated. It was just lips against lips. With some saliva thrown in to make things a little interesting. *Is this it? Is this what all the hype is about?*

As she got worked up, though, Melissa got creative. And she tossed me little hints:

"Bite on my lip, like this."

"Suck my bottom lip into your mouth."

"Suck on my neck right . . . there. Mmmm . . ."

As she started moaning and our breath became heavy, I was suddenly finding kissing a bit more interesting.

Right when I was getting into it, she stopped and pushed me away gently. I must have looked confused—which was appropriate, because I was. Why had she stopped? Had I done something wrong?

She put her hands on her thighs, drawing attention to her skirt.

"Look," she giggled as she flipped her skirt up. "No panties, just like I promised."

As she leaned over to resume our make-out session, she assertively placed my hand onto her wet vagina.

I wasn't quite sure what to do, so I just moved my hand up and down. Every now and then she let out a sharp moan, so I repeated whatever I had just done and assumed it was something she liked.

She stopped again. "Do you want to finger me?" she asked. I nodded.

She lay down across my lap and hiked up her skirt to give me easy access.

"Start with one finger. I'll tell you when to add more," she said.

I inserted my index finger and stuck it in gently. It was repulsive at first; the spongy inside of a vagina did not at all feel like I thought it would. But Melissa definitely responded to my finger thrusts. Her hips bucked up and down and she moaned fervently.

"Yeah . . . oh, yeah." Her voice was getting higher. "Put another finger in."

I complied.

"Oh yeah," she moaned. "Faster, faster, *faster*!"

I complied.

"Put another finger in!"

I complied.

I was getting into it. As my fingers thrust in and out of Melissa's vagina, I kissed her every now and then. But we couldn't get into a heavy make-out session, because her breath now came in ragged gasps. I thrust my fingers in and out as quickly as I could, and her excitement continued to escalate until, finally, her eyes rolled into the back of her head and she climaxed.

She crawled off my lap, gave me a sloppy kiss, and without a word undid my jeans, slid them to my ankles, and engulfed my penis in her mouth.

"Oh shit!" It was an incredible sensation. And while it was the best sexual sensation I'd had so far, I still found myself disappointed. Although my penis felt very warm and snug in her mouth, I wasn't being stimulated toward ejaculation. I wished she would use her tongue more, licking the head of my penis rather than bobbing her head up and down and focusing on the shaft, but again, my timidity stopped me from speaking up.

I became so uncomfortable that my erection began to fade. I panicked—what kind of pussy would I look like if I couldn't even keep it up when a woman was slobbering all over my cock? So, gently, I pulled her head away from my crotch, pushed her onto the back seat of the car and whispered into her ear, "Now it's *my* turn to taste *you*."

I spread her legs and paused. I was face to face with her vagina and we sat there staring at each other. I took a deep breath, and brought my mouth to her genitalia.

I was instantly wracked by more disappointment.

The taste was not at all pleasant. I knew it would be uncouth to gag while eating her out, so I stifled the instinct and continued running my tongue up and down the length of her slit. *Eh*, I thought, *maybe pussy is an acquired taste.*

Just as I was getting used to the taste, I paused to take a breath and noticed the distinct feeling of hair in my mouth. A pubic hair. From the muff I had just been munching. *Oh my goodness, I'm going to gag* . . .

But I didn't gag. I persisted. If I couldn't be pleased, then I would please, just as I had done my entire life. I'd always been the willing doormat, gladly letting people get their way while putting my own needs and desires on the backburner to make the people I cared about happy. My sex life was imitating my real life.

Melissa writhed and moaned, but she was nowhere near as enthralled with my tongue as she had been with my fingers—and I didn't want to go back to *that*, because my arms were as tired as if I'd been lifting weights.

Instead, I brought my pussy-juice-stained lips to hers and kissed her.

She brought her lips to my ear and whispered, "Do you want to stick it in . . . just for a minute?"

My heart raced. She was asking if I wanted to fuck her without a condom. I thought about it a moment. Maybe the reason I hadn't felt anything when I had sex with the hooker was because I'd worn a condom—maybe it had inhibited the sensation. If this girl was giving me the go-ahead to feel her from the inside, skin to skin, with no latex barrier, maybe I should try it.

On the other hand, the risks burned into my mind by my parents and sex education videos ate through my eagerness. What if this girl had a sexually transmitted disease? She seemed pretty easy; who knew how many guys she had been with? And after all, I'd had sex with a prostitute—what diseases might I give her if we had unprotected sex? I'd also heard that even if one used the "pull out" method of birth control, it was still possible to get a girl pregnant, because semen could leak out in one's precum. It could be enough to impregnate a woman. The last thing I needed was a baby with a girl I barely knew.

"Actually," I said, "I brought a condom."

Surprise overcame her face, but it quickly turned into a mischievous grin.

"Well, put it on," she said.

I got it out of the glove box, tore open the package, and fit it over my penis.

"Here we go," I said with a chuckle. I entered her and started thrusting. It was a bit uncomfortable in the cramped backseat of my car. That and several other factors all came together to undermine my confidence:

- I was worried that a drive-in employee would walk by, see the car shaking, and demand that we leave—or even call the police.
- Melissa wasn't reacting much to my fucking her. She had gone ape-shit with my fingers inside of her, but my penis apparently wasn't doing the trick.
- My dick still wasn't feeling anything
- My testicles were starting to ache—badly. I'd heard the term "blue balls" before, but this was the first time I'd ever experienced the phenomen firsthand. All this sexual stimulation without any release was like having someone squeeze my balls in a vice grip. Every thrust caused my balls to slap against her body, and each time it felt like someone had thrown a football into my groin.

Because of all this, my dick started going limp. I don't

think anyone who has never experienced trouble maintaining an erection can appreciate just how embarrassing—nay, how mortifying—it really is. *Here I am, a virile nineteen-year-old in decent shape and I can't even stay erect when I'm screwing a girl? I'm hard as a nail when I'm jerking off to internet porn, but when I have a real, live, actual woman writhing beneath me, her breath hot against my face, her snug, moist vagina wrapped tightly around my penis, I turn limp as a dishrag?*

It's enough to make one think they're gay.

I panicked and abruptly pulled out of her before I fully lost my rigor.

"Whew," I said.

"Did you come?"

"Um . . . yeah," I said. I pulled off the empty condom and wrapped it in a McDonald's napkin I found on the floor.

She wrapped her arms around my neck. I put mine around her waist. We kissed.

"This has been a really incredible night," I said. I meant it. Even though part of me was ashamed by what I'd just done, and another part was both disappointed and frustrated that this sexual encounter hadn't been everything I'd hoped it would be, my mind was nevertheless flooded with excitement.

It's a lesson that has stuck with me to this day: When an insecure guy like myself gets laid, he rides a wave of confidence that lasts at least a week. Having sex after a dry spell like that makes you feel like you could go up to any woman in the world and give her one of those grandiose, bend-her-backward kisses, and have her come up gasping for breath and giving you a look that made it apparent she wanted to bone your brains out. Of course, that would never actually happen, but whereas a despondent dry spell made such a prospect seem impossible, sex made it seem vaguely attainable.

I started buckling my belt while Melissa buttoned up her blouse.

"It really was a fun night," she said. "Too bad we didn't get to see the movie."

# Real College

All that we see or seem / Is but a dream within a dream.
—Edgar Allen Poe

I NEVER SAW MELISSA AGAIN.
She wasn't the kind of girl I was interested in getting involved with and I have a feeling I wasn't the kind of guy she was interested in either. I wanted an intelligent and scathingly funny girl; Melissa was a somewhat superficial, slightly dumb blonde. No doubt she wanted a confident, funny man; I was nervous and hesitant and too busy internally critiquing my every word to be very humorous.

That doesn't mean I gave up in my quest to find a girlfriend—or, failing that, another sex partner. In the meantime, I continued satisfying my carnal needs with pornography-fueled masturbation.

## Summer of Salvia

A major shift in my life gave me renewed hope that I could find a girlfriend. I had finished my two-year community college degree and was transferring to a university.

I felt confident that life at Eastern Oregon University in La Grande, Oregon, would be just what my life needed. If Hollywood had taught me anything, it was that college is the kind of hormone-driven cesspool of debauchery one can't *not* get laid in. I was guaranteed to, at the very least, find some wasted chick at a frat party to play tonsil hockey with. I had my reservations about leaving my hometown to attend college on the other side of the state, but those reservations were dwarfed by the immense anticipation I felt for my new life.

I decided to spend my first year living on campus in a dormitory. The promotional materials I'd received in the mail made dorm life sound pretty good. The university took care of internet, cable TV, water, and garbage; all I had to do was pay a quarterly fee to live there. Student loans would cover that.

My parents helped me load all my stuff up in their pickup and we set off for the university and the next chapter in my life.

It was in the high eighties in La Grande when we arrived. We walked into the dorm and checked in at the office. The office attendant gave me a key and a folder filled with university propaganda.

When I walked into the dorm I nearly had a heart attack.

There was no way this could be my dorm room. This was a *closet*. I must have stepped through the wrong door. But two beds and two desks sat on either side of the room, and there were two tiny closets against the wall.

This claustrophobic prison was going to be my home for the

next year.

I tried not to think about that as, with my parent's help, I hauled in all my belongings and tried to find places to fit it all into my new little dungeon.

While we were moving stuff in I noticed three people walking around outside—two guys and a girl. One of the guys was tall, had curly blonde hair and a somewhat muscular build. The other was shorter, but more muscular, and had dark hair. The girl was a petite brunette with a cute, delicate face.

As I wheeled in my mini-fridge on a hand truck, the blonde guy said, "Jason?"

I stopped the hand truck and turned around to face him.

"Yeah."

"Hi," he said, sticking out his hand for a handshake. "I'm Joel, your roomie."

"Oh, hi," I said, bringing my hand up to meet his. "Yeah, I'm just getting moved in. I see you already got all your stuff inside."

He nodded. "I've been here for two days," he said. He turned to the other guy and the girl. "This is my girlfriend, Jill," he said. "And this is Alex. He lives down the hall from us."

"Oh, do you guys know each other from back home?"

"No, we just met the other day," Alex said.

I suddenly felt very self-conscious. I was going to be roommates with a guy that had already made friends with people he'd only just met. How was I supposed to live up to that kind of confidence and social savvy?

"Well, nice to meet you guys," I said. "I'll talk to you later. I've still got a bunch of crap to move in."

"See you around," Joel said as he and his posse walked away.

I carted the mini fridge into my room and set it underneath

my bed while I went back for more stuff.

When we were done, I said goodbye to my parents and was left by myself, alone in a new, completely alien environment.

I immediately set to work organizing my room. It didn't take me long to get things generally organized. Joel came in halfway through and fiddled with his computer, then left.

It was late by the time I finished, so I made my bed, turned off the lights, crawled underneath the covers . . . and found a penis staring down at me from the ceiling.

Apparently, some smartass who had previously occupied the room thought it would be funny to arrange glow-in-the-dark stickers on the ceiling above my bed in the shape of a penis, complete with two large testicles. *Great*, I thought. *This is college life. This is what I have gotten myself into—two years of social ineptitude, pop quizzes, and penises watching me from above.* I was tired, so I decided to leave the dick on the ceiling; I'd take it down the next day.

That night, Joel came into the room and instinctively flipped the light switch after I'd settled into bed, although I hadn't yet fallen asleep.

"Sorry," he said and switched the lights back off.

"You can leave them on." There I went again—eager to please others, even to my own detriment.

"That's okay, I'm going to bed pretty soon myself."

He checked his email, then changed into boxers and a nightshirt and hopped onto his bed.

"So, where are you from?" he asked.

"Barlow. A little town in western Oregon. How about you?"

"I'm from Eugene."

"Ah, okay. I know where that is."

"Well, Jason," Joel said as he turned onto his side and wrapped his comforter snugly around his body, "it was nice to meet you. Sleep tight."

"You too."

THE NEXT MORNING I awoke to Joel calling my name.

"Jason. Jason!"

"Wh—what?" It took a few seconds for me to gain my bearings and remember I was in my new dorm room.

"Alex and I are going down to get our student ID cards, then we're gonna get some breakfast. You coming?"

"Now?"

"Yeah."

"Um . . ."

I didn't want to get my ID photo taken after I'd just woken up. But this *was* a good opportunity to be social, to be "one of the guys." I didn't want to insist on showering first; what if they got impatient and left without me?

"Yeah," I said. "Yeah, I'll come. Just let me get dressed." Joel and Alex stepped outside. I threw on a pair of pants, changed out of my nightshirt and met them outside in the hallway.

"Alright," I said. "Let's go."

We walked to the office where they handed out student ID cards. Joel and Alex went first, and as I stood there waiting for my turn, I regretted not grooming myself better. I couldn't see myself, but was sure I looked pretty gross. I'd been busy getting ready to pack for college and hadn't shaved in a couple days, so an ample amount of stubble covered my face. When I brought my hand to my hair, I could feel two or three tufts of hair sticking out, as if a herd of cows had gone to town licking my head while I slept. *Good lord, this is going to look even worse than my*

## Summer of Salvia

*driver's license photo.*

When they handed me my shiny new ID card, my worst fears were confirmed: I looked like the Unabomber.

"My photo looks pretty good," Joel said as he waved his visage toward us. "How'd your guys' turn out?"

"Mine's okay," Alex said and he showed the card to us.

"How about you?" Alex asked me.

"Mine turned out pretty bad," I said.

"I'm sure it's not that bad," Joel said. "Let's see it."

"I'd rather not."

"Oh, come on."

Reluctantly, I held up the card so they could see it.

Immediately, they both started laughing.

"You look like the Unabomber!" Joel choked out.

I started laughing too. Maybe it was amusing after all. Maybe my horrible student ID picture would be a good conversation starter.

"The Unabomber totally popped into my head, too!" I said. "It's not pretty, but I suppose it could be worse."

"Yeah," Joel said, "but not *much* worse."

WE ARRIVED AT the campus cafeteria closer to lunchtime than breakfast and I was delighted to see that, among dozens of other greasy offerings, the place served pizza. Joel and Alex seemed less impressed with cafeteria food dripping in grease, but this was just what I needed—soul food, to help fill the homesickness and anxiety plaguing my spirit.

Joel tinkered with his cell phone, then looked up at us. "Jill's going to be here in a second," he said.

"How did you guys meet?" I asked.

"High school. We're from the same town and we both decided to come here so we could stay together."

"Awww," Alex said with a cheesy grin. "Isn't that sweet?"

"Hey guys," Jill said as she approached and slid into the booth next to Joel. Her voice was soft but kind of husky and sexy. Now that I had the time to really study her, I found myself overwhelming attracted to her. I knew that was a road that would lead to immense awkwardness, so I suppressed my primal stirrings as best I could.

"Hi," Alex and I said in unison.

"Hey babe," Joel said and wrapped his arm around her shoulder.

They gave each other goo-goo eyes and acted like a typical, annoying couple—annoying to lonely single guys, anyway—so Alex and I excused ourselves and headed back to the dorm so they could publicly fondle each other without us trying to avert our gazes.

"Where are you from?" I asked Alex as we walked back to the dorm.

"Colorado," he said.

"What part?"

"Boulder."

"I've never been to Boulder, but I've been in Colorado."

"Boulder's great. It's a college town—the University of Colorado's there. So you can always find a party to crash. Over the summer, I was trashed more nights than not."

The conversation was making me a little uncomfortable. I had only ever been drunk once, and it had not been a fun experience. I hadn't even been with friends.

After high school, around the time I worked for FedEx, I swiped a bottle of whiskey from my uncle's liquor cabinet and mixed it with a bottle of Coca-Cola. I always thought I would be good and wait until I turned twenty-one to allow alcohol to pass through my lips. But I was lonely. I didn't really have any friends. I couldn't make any at school because I was always too nervous around people. Maybe alcohol was the solution, I thought. It was supposed to loosen people up.

So I experimented with my mixture of Coke and Whiskey, but I didn't feel any different at first. So I drank more. Gradually I started to feel the effects—and although I could tell I wasn't terribly drunk (my concoction was made up of more Coke than booze) it was also apparent that I was no longer sober.

I took a bus to Portland, positing that since my sobriety had been inhibited, I would be able to go up to people on the street and engage them in conversation, make all sorts of new friends, and maybe even enchant some beautiful young lass to take home and fuck.

I ended up walking around the streets by myself, a little frightened and frustrated that even after resorting to substance abuse, I still couldn't bring myself to talk to people (although I'm sure I would have looked like a total creep if I had). It turns out alcohol could impair my motor skills and my judgment, but not give me confidence or social skills! Who knew?

I took the bus back home and threw up in the bathtub, which turned out to be much harder to clean out than the toilet bowl would have been, as all the vomity chunks stuck to the sides, so I had to scrape them down to the drain. From that moment on, I decided drinking was not for me.

So as Alex told me of his drinking exploits in Colorado, I couldn't help but be both repulsed by his comments and drawn to them. On one hand, my brain warned me to stick to my convictions and abstain from drugs and alcohol, at least until I turned twenty-one, when it would be okay for me to treat myself to an occasional cocktail. On the other hand, my penis told me to stop being a wuss and go get drunk at a party, because there were bound to be hot, wasted chicks there that, as a result of their impaired judgment, would beg to have me inside them.

"I'm not a real big drinker," I told Alex.

He patted me on the back.

"You're in college now," he said. "You will be soon enough."

I scoffed at his words. Wasn't the stereotype that all college kids got drunk and partied just that—a stereotype? I could hold out. I could abstain from alcohol.

Little did I know that Alex was right.

# Self-Medication
# Part I: Alcohol

> If vision is the only validation, then most of my life isn't real. 'Cause if you're not really here, then the stars don't even matter. Now I'm filled to the top with fear, but it's all just a bunch of matter.
> —Sam Sparro, "Black and Gold"

THAT NIGHT, WHEN JOEL AND I TURNED OFF THE LIGHTS and crawled under our respective covers, we talked.

We talked about our hometowns and our experience with girls and school. The conversation turned to my belief in Christianity and, in turn, the sinfulness of cursing.

"I don't think swearing is a sin," I said. "The Bible doesn't say anything about it. I mean, it says something about 'clean speech,' but that's pretty vague."

"So you don't have any problem cussing?"

"I try not to cuss around people that would get offended by it. And I try not to cuss *at* people. And I don't take the Lord's name in vain. But it bugs the hell out of me that people get offended if you say 'shit' instead of 'poop.' They mean exactly the same thing! They're just words! It doesn't hurt a damn thing if you say 'shit' except someone's subjective sensibilities."

It was the first time Joel and I had talked in depth. It was the first inkling of friendship and I got the feeling that Joel and I were going to be great friends.

JILL LIVED A floor above us and her roommate, Amanda, had moved out of the dorms and into an apartment with her boyfriend. She invited Jill and Joel to go to a small "housewarming" party they were having. Joel asked if I wanted to join them.

I did, but I felt a little awkward since I hadn't been directly invited. But I was desperate to participate in social activities and make friends, so I agreed to go.

Joel, Jill and I walked together to the apartment, which wasn't too far from our dorm. As we entered, I found it smaller than I'd anticipated, although I had to admit, it was still a world roomier than the dorms. The living area was rather small, but enough for the seven people in attendance (Amanda, her boyfriend Chris, her sister Amy, Amy's boyfriend Tom, Joel, Jill, and me). There was also a small bathroom and a small bedroom, and a little kitchen off to the side of the living area. It wasn't much, but it looked like Amanda and Chris had already made it a home.

"Hey man, what's up?" Chris said to Joel, shaking his hand. He turned to me and reached out his hand. "Hi," he said.

"Hi," I said and shook his hand. "I'm Jason, Joel's roommate."

## Part I: Alcohol

"Nice to meet you."

"You too."

The living room was set up with a TV against the wall with a couch facing it, and two chairs on either side of the couch. Joel and I sat down on the couch while Jill and Amanda hung around the kitchen area, poured themselves drinks and gossiped.

Chris sat down on the chair beside the couch with two cans of Bud Light sparkling blue and silver. He handed one to Joel and then held the other up to me.

"Want one?"

"Sure," I said. Okay, maybe I wouldn't be holding out until I was twenty-one, but this was certainly an opportunity for me to drink responsibly. And hopefully it would help me loosen up, because I was sitting on this couch rigid as a board, too nervous to say anything to anyone.

I popped the can, brought it to my lips, and tasted beer for the first time.

I tried my best not to grimace. It literally tasted like piss (and don't ask me how I knew that). But I didn't want to look like a novice drinker—even though I was one—so I politely took a sip every now and then.

Chris picked up an Xbox 360 controller and started playing a racing game.

"Anyone else want to play?" he asked after several minutes of playing by himself.

"I'll play you," Joel said. "And I'll kick your ass!"

They embroiled themselves in virtual combat, shooting snide comments at each other all the while. Jill and Amanda continued gossiping in the kitchen, and Amy and Tom left, probably to buy more beer. I was left on the couch with nobody to talk to, watching Chris and Joel have fun as they engaged in an actual social interaction. I felt like I was failing at my effort to be more sociable, which made me more nervous, which made me more withdrawn.

I looked down at the beer in my hand. I stared it down for a good, long minute. A debate raged in my head. I tried to decide whether I should pace myself or if it would really help me to just down the whole can and have another.

I brought the can to my mouth and took a hefty gulp.

I couldn't bring myself to finish the rest of the can in one sitting. But I finished it quickly, in two or three massive sips, and then walked to the kitchen to get another.

I felt a little funny, but not too different. I was reminded of my experiment with whiskey and coke before my outing in Portland.

The girls finished talking and convinced Joel and Chris to forego their game and put on *The Incredibles*. I sipped my beer. Everyone else got up and socialized every now and then, glancing at the movie during their favorite parts. I was the only one that sat glued to the couch and watched the whole movie. I pretended to be entranced by it so I didn't have to talk to anyone.

At one point I got up to use the bathroom. As I emptied my bladder, I heard the girls talking in the kitchen. They were talking about me, apparently unaware how small the apartment was and how thin the walls were.

"Jason looks like he's sick or something. I don't think he usually drinks."

"He's so quiet! What is wrong with him?"

"I think he's just shy."

"I feel kind of bad for him."

When I walked out of the bathroom, I pretended like I hadn't heard their exchange.

## Part I: Alcohol

At the end of the night, I looked at my two empty beer cans and couldn't help but think, *Maybe I just wasn't drunk enough.*

I DIDN'T TALK to anyone in any of my classes. Usually, I sat by myself and read a newspaper while I waited for class to start.

Psychology 101 was a large class, held in a huge, rotunda-style classroom with auditorium-style seating.

I sat down on the end of a row and pulled my newspaper out of my backpack, when a girl sat down next to me.

I studied her out of the corner of my eye. There was plenty of room further down the aisle, numerous empty seats. But she chose to sit directly next to me.

My heart pounded.

"Hi."

I turned to look at her.

Both her body and face were petite and her silky black hair cascaded elegantly past her shoulders. She looked fashionable, sporting a red, velvet jacket, black leggings beneath a dark skirt, and brown boots. She was cute.

That made me nervous.

"Hi," I said, surprised my voice didn't crack.

"Whatcha reading?"

"Um. Uh. The newspaper." Duh. She was obviously making small talk.

"Anything interesting?"

"Yeah, actually. A couple interesting articles. But then, there's always something worth reading."

"Yeah," she said. "Definitely."

Even her voice was soft and cute. What was this girl doing, talking to me?

"Are you a freshman?" she asked.
"No, I'm a transfer student. You?"
"I'm a freshman."
"Cool. Do you live here in La Grande?"
She shook her head and I felt I might drown in adorability.
"Actually, I live in Pendleton with my sister."
"Damn, that's quite a commute."
She shrugged.
"The rent's free, so that makes up for the gas."
"Are you from Pendleton originally?"
"I'm from New York."
"Whoa."

I'd already set my hopes ridiculously high. This girl had only been sitting next to me for five minutes—class hadn't even started yet—and I was already gauging whether she was potential girlfriend material, and whether, when we were both done with school, she would be able to relocate to Salem to settle down and raise a family with me.

I felt like a middle-aged woman with an expiring biological clock. My thoughts made no sense, yet I couldn't help thinking them.

Class started, so she didn't have a chance to tell me how a New Yorker ended up in a small college in eastern Oregon. I made a mental note to ask her the next time I saw her.


THERE WAS ONE problem: I couldn't remember what she looked like.

Some people like to make a point of telling their friends, "I never remember a name, but I never forget a face."

Unfortunately, I never remember a name *or* a face. She hadn't

## Part I: Alcohol

given me her name yet, but I should have been able to recognize her face.

I couldn't.

It was a big class, and I saw two or three girls that could have been her. I didn't want to mistakenly start talking to the wrong girl only to have the original overhear and dismiss me as a lusty rake. So I sat in my seat and didn't talk to anybody. I waited for her to talk to me.

But she didn't sit next to me in the next class. When I scanned the rows of seats behind me, I was pretty sure I saw her sitting in the row above me, though I couldn't be certain. I sure as hell wasn't going to move and go sit next to her. It would seem aggressive. Everyone in the class would look at me and judge me as I moved my things next to her. They'd all say to themselves, "Look at that loser. Does he seriously think he has a chance with that chick? It's *so* obvious he's into her, but she has no interest at all in him!"

She didn't sit next to me during the next class either, and I decided I'd blown it and it had only been a fluke that she'd talked to me in the first place. Perhaps she had merely spoken to me out of boredom, or to make some other guy in class jealous. Or maybe she was just waiting for me to act like a guy with a pair of balls and talk to *her* first. Although I had a very nice pair of testicles between my legs, I was completely lacking the metaphorical kind that symbolize boldness and masculine assertiveness.

Then a miracle happened. I walked into class one day and sat down. Soon thereafter, *she* sat down in the seat next to me. At least, I was pretty sure it was her.

"Hi," I said. That was noncommittal enough; if it was the same girl, she'd merely think I was saying "Hi," as in, "Why, hello again, old friend!" If it was a different girl, she'd just think I was striking up a conversation.

"Hi," she replied. "How'd you do on the test last week?"

"I did okay," I said. "I think I got an 87 or something."

"I got an 84."

"Not bad. We both got B's."

"So, I never asked you the other day what your name was."

"You're right," I said, "You didn't." I laughed.

"Well . . . what is it?" she said, also laughing.

"Jason Cole. What's yours?"

"Roxy Phillips."

"Wait . . . are you serious?"

"Yeah," she said. "It's kind of embarrassing."

"You shouldn't be embarrassed. That's an awesome name. I can say with ninety-nine percent certainty you are the only Roxy I know."

"Well that's true," she said. "It is unique. But that can be a blessing and a curse sometimes. The kids were not at all shy when it came to teasing me about it."

"Yeah, well, kids are pricks. Well, sometimes. You know what I mean."

She laughed. "Yes, I know what you mean. Some kids are just bullies."

"I hate to judge too much. Who knows what they were dealing with at home? Their parents probably beat them or something, so they took it out on the smaller kids." I sighed. "The world can be a cruel place."

"Yeah," said Roxy. "But it can be a very beautiful place as well."

As we spoke, I felt myself falling in love with Roxy Phillips. By the end of the day, I was daydreaming about what our wedding would be like.

I was happy because I was hopeful my daydreams would come

## Part I: Alcohol

true. And I was terrified because I knew that in all likelihood they would not.

Roxy and I became fairly good friends. But she was making other friendships, too, back in Pendleton. I couldn't help but feel a little jealous. I visited her in Pendleton sometimes. But because of the distance, I could only make the trip on select weekends.

One day I ran into Roxy on campus and she handed me a slip of folded-up paper.

"What's this?"

"An invitation."

I opened it up.

"An invitation to what?" I asked. As I studied the skulls artfully painted on the inside of the invitation, Roxy explained.

"It's a Halloween party I'm throwing with some of my friends in Pendleton," she said. "It's not actually on Halloween, it's two days before."

I grew excited. I was being invited to a party! A real, live college party with booze and girls and music! Maybe I was about to start experiencing the social benefits college is all about. Maybe I was about to start living my life instead of standing still while it moved about me, like one of those moving sidewalks in airports.

"Will you come?"

"Um . . . yeah, I guess."

"Great," she said with a wide grin. She walked away, then turned her head over her shoulder. "One more thing—make sure you wear a costume."

Great. I was going to have to come up with a cool costume, which was pretty much impossible for me.

When I got back to the dorm, I looked online for costume

ideas. Many sites sold pre-made costumes but they were all expensive. I didn't feel like going as Spiderman or something anyway. Too pedestrian.

I felt frustrated. I couldn't think of a good costume idea, so I finally decided to get my hands on some fake blood, pour a bunch on my forehead, and tell people that was my costume.

On the day of the party, I did just that. I messed up my hair to make it look like I'd gotten into a fight or something, then smeared blood on my forehead and across my face. I climbed into my car and headed for Pendleton.

I got lost, like I usually do, but finally found the place after a few minutes of driving aimlessly around the general vicinity. The party was at Roxy's friend Greg's house.

The place was a dump, but that wasn't surprising considering it was occupied by a college kid. Old brown, shag carpet lined the floors and the walls were made of old wood paneling. The place seemed spacious enough, with a little living room, a full kitchen, two bathrooms and three bedrooms. Everyone was hanging out upstairs, but I was informed the party would eventually be moved to the basement.

When I arrived, I could count the number of attendees on one hand. It was exactly what I had feared most. If there were only a few people here, they would not be mingling. They would form little self-contained groups and talk amongst themselves and I would be left out because I didn't know anyone except Roxy.

That's exactly what happened. Everyone had someone to talk to except me. I hated this feeling. All I could do was slowly walk through the house, pretending to study the pictures on the wall, or the molding around a door, so it seemed like I was merely fascinated by my surroundings rather than just too shy to make friends with any of these strangers.

## Part I: Alcohol

*Dear Lord, where's the booze? Where's Roxy?*

If I could get drunk, maybe it would be less painful to go up and talk to someone. If Roxy were here, at least I'd be able to talk to her briefly before she made her rounds to visit all her guests.

I picked up a little ceramic cat figurine—and I genuinely was a little curious what something like that was doing in a house like this—when the front door burst open, and Roxy walked in, accompanied by two other girls and a guy. The guy carried a large, brown paper bag. Suddenly, the whole house came alive. I'm not sure if it was because Roxy had arrived, or the booze had arrived, or both.

Everyone came up to Roxy and greeted her, giving her hugs and bullshitting with her. I waited in the corner for the bedlam to die down a bit before going up to her and tapping her on the shoulder.

"Hey, Roxy," I said.

"Jason!" she squealed. "I'm so glad you came!" She wrapped her arms around my neck. I awkwardly wrapped one of my arms around her and patted her on the back.

"Yep," I said, "I made it. So . . ."

"Roxy!" someone behind me shouted.

"Devin! What's up?" she said, and slugged Devin playfully on the shoulder. I looked up at him. He was a good-looking guy, with blonde, semi-spiky hair, a prominent chin and . . . ugh . . . dimples. Handsome bastard. The twin emotions of despair and sorrow flooded me, along with jealousy and an overwhelming sense of inadequacy.

"Hey Roxy! Come over here!" One of the girls shouted from across the room.

"Excuse me," Roxy said to us and she walked away.

I turned to the guy standing beside me, ready to make small

talk, but he was already walking away to join his friends. I was left standing alone once again. Jason Cole, always the awkward outsider.

My breath came out ragged and a little frantic. Every second that passed by with me standing by myself made me more anxious. Fearing I was about to have a panic attack, I walked to the couch, sat down and tried to slow my breathing.

Not even a minute after I sat down, Roxy announced that everyone should head downstairs, where someone had set up the alcohol into a little bar.

I hurried downstairs and walked to the "bar," which was actually a card table with several bottles of cheap booze sitting on it, along with a stack of plastic cups, a couple shot glasses, and a few 2-liter bottles of Coke and 7-Up for mixer. Apparently, anyone that preferred beer was shit out of luck. That was fine. I hated beer. I hated hard liquor, too, but I figured I'd look hardcore if I downed a couple of shots.

I walked to the table and poured a shot of Canadian Whiskey. I counted to three (as I always did before I took a shot—it was just like preparing myself to take a shot of grape-flavored cough syrup when I was little). I brought the glass to my lips, tilted back my head, and let the burning liquid slide down my throat.

I tried my hardest not to grimace. Good heavens, liquor tasted terrible. I sat down on the couch and watched as everyone from upstairs flooded into the basement, talking and laughing and—as Roxy and her friend Amber put on some music—dancing. I was doing none of the above. I got up and walked back to the liquor table.

I wasn't feeling anything yet so I took another shot—rum this time. I still wasn't feeling anything, so I figured maybe I'd better take another shot for good measure. I set down the shot glass

## Part I: Alcohol

and walked back to the couch, but this time I didn't sit down. I figured if I stood, people would assume I was open to talking to them, even though I wasn't. I definitely wasn't going to have the courage to talk to anyone. The best I could hope for was that they would talk to me.

And they did. Some Michael Jackson song came on and Amber, who I'd met a couple times, turned to me and said, "Come on Jason, let's dance."

She and Roxy were getting their groove on and I just gave a pathetic little half-smile and said, "Uh . . . I'm not really much of a dancer." It was freaking middle school all over again. Six years, and I still hadn't made any progress. I still couldn't dance, I still couldn't talk to people and I still couldn't make friends (close friends, anyway). I was a fucking loser. I'd always been a loser and I always would be.

I walked back to the liquor and took two more shots.

I was starting to feel the effects of the alcohol now, but I still didn't feel drunk. I shrugged, poured some more whiskey, and took one last shot.

I felt a little funny, but I didn't feel drunk. I must have looked pale or something, though, because Roxy came up to me, her eyebrows raised with concern.

"Are you okay, Jason? You don't look so good."

"Yeah," I said. "I'm fine."

"Are you sure?"

"Yeah," I said. "I'm—"

That's when the six shots I'd taken caught up with me. I shifted my weight from one leg to the other and collapsed onto the floor.

"Oh man, I'm sorry!" I said as I came to my feet. "Sorry, sorry!"

"Are you okay?"

"I . . . I think I'm going to throw up."

I walked to the stairwell but I couldn't make my way up the stairs—I kept stumbling. I had to get on all fours and crawl up them.

Roxy helped me up the stairs and to the bathroom.

"I didn't realize how much I was drinking," I said apologetically. My words came out slurred but I barely noticed. "I'm really, really, *really* sorry about this. I'm so sorry if I ruined your party."

She laughed. "Jason, you didn't ruin it."

Then I blacked out.

I WOKE UP on the couch later that night. I tried to remember how I'd gotten there. The last thing I remembered vividly was crawling up the stairs, but I had vague, mercurial memories of sitting in front of the toilet, confident my nausea was going to pass and that I wasn't going to vomit. Then images came into my head of my lunch shooting out my mouth and splattering the white porcelain with yellowish-brown chunks of guck.

I sat up on the couch and looked around. Two guys and two girls sat on another couch and a chair, watching television. It took me a minute, but as I identified the actors—Kevin Spacey, Chris Cooper, Annette Bening—I realized they were watching *American Beauty*. I'd never seen it before, but it won a bunch of awards when it came out, so I'd heard all about it. I sat and stared as Annette Bening's character, standing in the midst of a downpour, screamed at the top of her lungs.

"This movie is weird," I said.

My movie companions looked startled. They hadn't realized I'd woken up.

"You came to," one of the girls said. She was skinny and had

## Part I: Alcohol

kind of a hipster look going on. She wore skinny jeans and converse shoes with a gray flannel jacket, and had a beanie wrapped around her head.

"Yeah," I said. "I'm not really sure what happened. I guess I drank too much."

"Uh, yeah," the girl said. "You definitely drank too much." She paused, then added, "You were really funny."

"I was?"

"Yeah. You're a fun drunk."

I thought about that. I realized that before that night, I had never truly been drunk. I had been intoxicated, I had been buzzed, I had "felt it," but I had never been *drunk*. I'd certainly never been blackout drunk until then.

Maybe alcohol was the solution to my problems after all.

# Middle School Revisited

> I have realized that the past and future are real illusions, that they exist in the present, which is what there is and all there is.
> —Alan W. Watts

MySpace, the infamous social networking website, was immensely popular when I was in college. Facebook wouldn't really take off for another year or two.

I'd heard stories of friends reconnecting with old classmates via MySpace, so I figured I'd try to reconnect with some of mine.

One of the people I messaged was Veronica, the girl I'd had a crush on in the eighth grade.

I was surprised when she seemed more than happy to talk to me. Some of the other people I'd messaged chose to ignore me, and I couldn't blame them. I'd been pretty weird in middle school.

Frankly, I'm still a little weird.

What surprised me more was that she messaged me back with her phone number.

We texted back and forth a little, but didn't really connect until she called me late one night. It was the first time we'd ever talked on the phone.

"Hello?"

"Hey. Jasooon!"

"Veronica?"

"Jasooon!"

"Veronica . . . what are you doing?"

There was a long silence on the phone and I could hear her either sighing or breathing heavily.

"I'm sorry, Jason. I'm tripping on 'shrooms hardcore right now."

I couldn't help but laugh.

"You are?"

"Don't laugh! It's not funny. I'm with my friend in Portland and we both decided to do 'em, but I think I took too much because I am seriously tripping balls right now. It's actually kind of cool. But it's scary."

"What's happening right now? Are you hallucinating? Are you seeing things?"

"Nah, I'm not really seeing anything out of the ordinary. It's just that everything is so . . . sparkly . . . all over. I don't even know how to describe it. It's like everything is covered in glitter."

I laughed again. Psychedelic mushrooms were one drug I *wasn't* willing to try, but it was fun to experience them vicariously through Veronica.

"It's been fun, but it's getting late," I said. "I'll leave you to have fun with your friend."

"Alright. I'll call you some other time, Jasey-wasey."

"Okay," I said. "And don't ever call me that again."

We talked on the phone a lot after that. It was hard for me to fathom. Here was the girl I'd had the biggest crush on in middle school talking to me and even flirting with me a little.

The more we talked, the more she brought up the prospect of meeting up in person. Winter break was quickly approaching, so I'd be back in western Oregon. Veronica lived in Portland, which wasn't too far away from my hometown. We made plans to meet downtown. She wanted to show me a Filipino place she liked, since she was half Filipino herself.

"Look who it is," I said as she walked up to the restaurant.

"Who is it?" She asked.

"A hot girl," I said. "She's standing behind you, Veronica, off in the distance . . ."

She laughed and hit me on the arm. I didn't understand why I was so comfortable around her, but I wasn't complaining.

"Let's eat," she said. She darted into the restaurant and I followed behind her.

It was soon apparent that what was supposed to be old middle school friends reconnecting was actually a date. There was a flirtatious vibe in the air, and at the end of dinner, I knew I wanted to see her again.

It was all a bit confusing, because I still had a secret crush on Roxy. But not only was I not sure Roxy was into me, I'd begun to feel like we were growing apart. Veronica, on the other hand, seemed totally into me. Dating her would allow me to fulfill my adolescent middle school fantasies.

We went out for pizza the next weekend.

I picked her up at her apartment this time. "Come on in," she said. "I want to show you something."

I followed her into her bedroom and she beckoned me to her

computer. She showed me some internet cartoons she thought were funny and, eager to outdo her, I showed her some of my favorite cartoons from the webcomic *Toothpaste for Dinner*.

"Okay, okay," I said. "This is fun, but I'm starving. Let's go eat."

"I don't want to go yet," she said. She walked a few feet and sat down on her bed, a pouty look on her face. "I'm having fun here."

"You sound awfully whiny," I said as I walked toward her, "and whiners get . . . *tickled!*" I started tickling her sides, surprised by my own spontaneity.

She squealed and squirmed, collapsing into a gyrating mess of giggles. But she was feisty, and she returned my barrage with tickles of her own. I was briefly reminded of my tickle war with Melissa at the drive-in theater, the night I lost my virginity. Scratch that: the night I had sex for the first time without paying for it.

Once the giggling died down, we left for pizza.

As we walked from the parking lot into the restaurant, she turned to me and said, "You know, you're really quite cute."

"That is a horrible, horrible thing to tell a guy," I said. "No guy wants to be called cute. From now on, you're only allowed to call me a hot stud."

She couldn't contain her laughter. "Oh yeah?" she said. "Well then, you're a *hot stud*. I'll just say that whenever I think you're being cute!"

"No! That totally defeats the purpose!"

"Oh, whatever, you *hot stud*."

From that moment on, we started acting like a couple.

## Middle School Revisited

A WEEK LATER, Veronica moved into a new apartment and decided to throw a housewarming party. She invited me.

I hung out with her prior to the party as she drove around town gathering supplies: plastic cups, beer, napkins, beer, limes, beer . . .

As people showed up to the apartment, the witty banter I'd exchanged so easily with Veronica ran dry. I didn't know any of the other people she'd invited and I always found it difficult to establish rapport with friends of friends (or friends of girlfriends) that I barely knew.

I started sucking down a beer right away. Then another. And another.

I got the spins.

"I'm going to go lie down in your bed," I told Veronica. "I don't feel well."

She came in several times to check on me. She seemed genuinely concerned, but I assured her I was fine.

"Go enjoy your party," I said.

She went out for a little while and then came back in. It seemed like mere minutes, but it must have been at least an hour.

"Everyone left," she said. "And you are staying here tonight. Because you obviously cannot drive home."

I was too drunk to protest.

"Let's get these off of you," she said as she unfastened my belt.

"W—what? No! Veronica, don't."

"You are not going to sleep in my bed with your jeans on."

"I'll go crash on the couch."

"Nonsense," she said with a giggle. "You're going to sleep with me. Now let's get you out of your panties."

"Don't call them pan—oh! Veronica, Veronica, Veronica!" I squealed, fighting to keep my pants on. "I—I don't feel comfortable getting, you know, sexual with you. I mean . . ."

"Okay, okay," she said. "I promise we don't have to get sexual, but you are cuddling with me at the very least. You'll be more comfortable if you take off your pants. I promise I won't take advantage."

"Alright . . ." I said hesitantly. "I'll take them off."

I gently pushed her away, and removed them myself. I crawled under her covers, clothed in a T-shirt and boxers, and she slid in beside me, wearing only her bra and panties.

It was my first time spooning and I loved it. I let the scent of her hair wash over me and slid my hand down her shoulder and across her thighs.

"This is nice," I said.

"It is," she whispered.

Then the alcohol overwhelmed us and we both passed out.

When I returned to La Grande, I started sexting with Veronica before the term even existed.

As my relationship with Veronica became more serious, I realized it wasn't taking place in a bubble.

Who is this girl? Roxy asked me in a text message. She'd seen comments Veronica had posted on my MySpace profile. Jason, this girl is, like, in LOVE with you!

Fuck. If there had been *any* chance of getting together with Roxy, I'd blown it. She now considered me taken. And Veronica was such a sure thing, I couldn't bring myself to ditch her.

Veronica and I made plans to meet again when I was home on spring break. She wanted to *go* somewhere. Have a mini vacation. I told her I couldn't afford that.

"I can help pay," she said on the phone. She worked in a

nursing home, and while she wasn't exactly rolling in money, she was making more than I was, since I was just living off student loans.

"Okay," I said. "It's a deal."

I decided we'd spend the weekend at the ocean.

I looked up motels online, trying to find the cheapest one possible. After calling dozens, I finally found one for just forty-five bucks a night, which sounded like a good deal to me.

The motel was housed in an old brick building with a winding staircase that led to our room.

A Queen-size bed sat by the window. Just to the left of the doorway, a futon sat against the wall.

"Sweet!" I said, setting my backpack on the futon. "Dibs!"

"You are *not* sleeping on that couch," Veronica said indignantly. "If you don't sleep in the bed with me, we're not staying."

It didn't seem worth it to argue with her.

We walked down to the beach. It was cool, but not cold, and the crashing waves accompanied by the endless sand canvas stretching before us set a romantic mood. I grabbed Veronica's hand and saw her smile out of the corner of my eye.

We headed back into town and ate dinner at a Mexican restaurant. Mexican wasn't my favorite, but Veronica and I had argued over where to eat and Mexican was the best compromise we could come up with. I ordered two beers to wash everything down.

Afterward, we headed back to the motel. I hopped onto the futon. Veronica walked past me and sat on the edge of the bed.

"Nuh-uh," she said. "Remember what I said? You come in this bed with me or I'm going to leave you here by yourself."

I was too buzzed from the beer to argue. I took off my pants and slid under the covers while she undressed. Wearing only her bra and panties, she slid in beside me.

I wrapped my arms around her and looked into her eyes. Our lips met. They met again. The next thing I knew, we were attacking each other with our lips, ferociously kissing each other as if we were cannibals.

She pulled off my shirt and I didn't protest. I kissed her breasts through her bra. I reached to unfasten it. After several unsuccessful attempts, she reached behind and undid it herself.

I brought my mouth to her breasts, ran my tongue around her nipple and squeezed her other breast.

"I want you inside me," she breathed into my ear.

I was done resisting. I was done being Mr. Nice Guy. I wanted to fuck the shit out of Veronica Keith, just as I'd always dreamt of doing in middle school.

I pulled off my boxers and stuck my hand inside her panties, running my fingers along her vaginal lips as we kissed.

"That feels amazing," she said.

"You feel so wet," I said.

"You made me that way," she responded. "I want you inside me *now*, Jason."

I was about to rip her panties off and go for it, when I remembered reading online somewhere about the importance of foreplay before sex.

"Do you . . . do you want me to go down on you first?"

A look of disgust came over her face.

"No. Gross." Her face grew serene again. "I want your cock inside me, Jason."

"I need a condom," I said.

She nodded. I retrieved one from my pants pocket (I really hadn't intended to sleep with her, but I'd taken the motto "be prepared" seriously), and slid it over my penis.

## Middle School Revisited

I had trouble sliding it in at first, which was embarrassing. She grabbed my dick herself and guided it into her.

It felt amazing at first, so warm and snug. Veronica moaned into my ear and we kissed while I thrust in and out of her.

My penis began hurting. It felt like it was bending with each thrust. In hindsight, I don't think she was lubricated enough for penetration. I wish I had insisted on more foreplay.

Only adding to the discomfort, as I continued thrusting, I got blue balls; a sharp pain shot through my testicles each time they slapped against her. After about ten minutes, I had to stop. I apologized and wrapped my arms around her as we lay side by side.

"I think you're the perfect size for me," she said in my arms. "And you almost gave me an orgasm."

I didn't take that as a compliment.

ALTHOUGH WE'D BEEN acting a lot like a couple during my winter break, I'd made it clear to Veronica from the beginning that our little tryst would only last until I went back to school.

The weekend before I left, we sat together in my car after sharing a dinner at Applebees.

"I know we said this was going to be temporary," she told me, looking out the passenger side window. "But I like you so much. We're so compatible. I know your school's far away, but I can come see you on weekends."

I didn't know what to say. I didn't want Veronica coming to see me on weekends—I wanted to go to parties on the weekends and try my damndest to pick up chicks. I wanted to live a life of crazy casual sex. Or at least die trying.

But I didn't want to break her heart.

"Sure," I said. Our eyes met. "Let's give it a try."

## Summer of Salvia

Alex invited me to a frat party the same weekend Veronica planned her first visit. He'd been hanging out with a couple people from the fraternity and was becoming a frequent presence at their parties.

"There's a party at my friend's frat," I told her on the phone. "You want to go with me, meet some of my friends?"

"Sure, sounds like fun."

When she arrived, we got some dinner, then drove to the frat house together.

We were early and only a half dozen people were there. Half of them surrounded the pool table where two young, attractive women were engaged in a match. Alex sat on a stool watching them, a small, petite woman sitting on his lap—his girlfriend of a couple weeks, Emily.

"Hey," I said as we approached. "How's it going?"

"It's going good," he said, sounding completely complacent and not at all excited.

"Alex, this is my girlfriend, Veronica. Veronica, this is my friend Alex and his girlfriend Emily."

Head nods were exchanged.

I fetched a couple beers. Veronica and I watched the two girls duke it out on the pool table, neither of them saying much to each other.

It didn't take ten minutes for her to lean into my ear and whisper, "I'm bored. Let's go."

"The party hasn't even started," I whispered. "Things will pick up."

The party picked up, but we didn't.

People streamed through the doors as the night went on, but Alex had gone off with Emily somewhere, and while I ran into a couple people I knew here and there, nobody stuck around long enough for a decent conversation. Veronica and I ended up on a couch together, trying to talk over the music, which was now blasting through the house.

"Now can we go?" she asked, exasperated.

I was frustrated, both by my lack of social connections and by her impatience.

"Fine," I yelled into her ear annoyedly. "Let's get the fuck out of here."

We went back to my dorm room and lay down on my bed. Joel wasn't in yet. We kissed each other fervently and let our hands roam over each other's bodies.

When Veronica unbuttoned my jeans, I placed my hands on hers to stop her.

"No," I said. I was afraid Joel might walk in and I didn't want him to see me naked. Or to see us having sex, for that matter.

"What do you mean, 'No?'" she asked, annoyed.

"No sex tonight," I said. "Not here."

"You don't want to have sex with me?"

"No," I said. I should have explained why, but I didn't.

"Fine."

I put my arm around her and she shrugged it off. I tried again. Same reaction.

"Baby..."

She rolled over toward the wall so her back was facing me.

"Baby, talk to me," I said. "Let me explain."

"I'm going to sleep," she said sternly.

I rolled over facing the opposite direction and closed my eyes.

THE NEXT MORNING we went to the mall and the fighting continued. Every petty little thing set her off. It hadn't lasted long, but I decided I'd already had enough of this relationship.

When we got back to my dorm, we stood outside talking on the sidewalk.

"This is clearly not working," I said.

"You think we should break up?" she asked.

"Yes."

"Yeah," she said, looking down at her feet. "Maybe you're right." Her distress seemed minimal.

"Maybe we can give it a try when I'm done with school," I said. "In the meantime, we can still be friends."

"I'd like that," she said.

We hugged. I kissed her on the cheek, then she got in her car and left.

A couple months later, after she'd stopped responding to my texts, I read on MySpace that she'd gotten married and had a baby on the way.

Shortly after that, she deleted me from her MySpace profile and my first adult relationship officially came to an end.

# Self-Medication
# Part II: Marijuana

> [T]here is no God, no universe, no human race, no earthly life, no heaven, no hell. It is all a dream—a grotesque and foolish dream. Nothing exists but you. And you are but a thought—a vagrant thought, a useless thought, a homeless thought, wandering forlorn among the empty eternities!
> —MARK TWAIN, *The Mysterious Stranger*

"HAVE YOU EVER SMOKED POT?"

I thought back to my experience with Katie, when we'd attempted to play pool while stoned.

"Once. I didn't really like it."

"Really?" Joel asked incredulously, as if it was unheard of for a college student to not enjoy getting high. "Why not?"

"I don't know. It just made me feel really weird, really different.

It's not healthy, anyway."

"It's safer than alcohol," Joel said. I'd noticed that he could get pretty stubborn, and every once in a while he seemed to start an argument just for the sake of arguing.

"It can't be good to smoke it, though," I said. "It's not good to smoke *anything* into your lungs."

"Let's say that's true. What if you eat it? You know, bake it into some brownies or something. What harm does that do?"

"Well, I guess it wouldn't do any harm, then."\*

"Exactly. It just mellows you out. There's no reason it should be illegal if alcohol is legal. Alcohol kills a lot more people than marijuana. Marijuana doesn't kill anyone."†

"Yep, you're right," I said. It wasn't worth arguing with him when he got this stubborn.

Later that week, Alex invited me to another frat party. When I asked Joel if he wanted to go, I was surprised by his reaction.

"I don't hang out with Alex anymore," he said.

"Did something happen?"

"I don't want to talk about it," he said coldly.

"Okay . . . well you could still go and just avoid him."

"I don't want to be in the same room as that bastard."

I wasn't going to miss out on this party, whether Joel was mad at Alex or not. Later that night, Alex and I walked together to the frat house.

"Did something happen between you and Joel?" I asked.

"What do you mean?"

---

\* That isn't exactly true. I'm far from a cannabis prohibitionist, but marijuana certainly does carry risks, even if eaten instead of smoked. Studies show it can cause infertility, for example, and it can trigger psychosis in predisposed individuals. But I didn't know that at the time.

† On this point, he was unequivocally correct. #LegalizeIt

## Part II: Marijuana

"I asked if he wanted to come tonight and he seemed really mad at you."

Alex grimaced.

"It probably has to do with the fact that I slept with Jill."

"You slept with his *girlfriend*? No wonder he's pissed at you!"

"I know, I know," Alex said. "But technically they were broken up at the time."

Joel and Jill had developed an on-and-off again relationship since arriving in La Grande. It seemed Joel was torn between spreading his new wings of freedom at college (and in his bed), and the frequent companionship (and sex) a steady girlfriend afforded him.

"Does that really make a difference?" I asked.

"It does to me, but apparently it doesn't to him" he said, "He thinks I should have asked his permission, even after they'd broken up." He shook his head. "As if that wouldn't have been the most awkward conversation of my life."

"Are they back together now?"

"Not that I know of."

"Sorry I brought it up. Let's just go enjoy the party."

"Yeah," he said excitedly. "We are going to get so shitfaced!"

I'd been debating whether I should drink much at this party. On one hand, I didn't like how little control I'd had after downing six shots at Roxy's Halloween party. On the other hand, I had been called a fun drunk and that made the prospect of getting drunk again very tempting. Even blacking out and doing things I couldn't remember somehow appealed to me. In a weird way, it made me feel like I was living out the movie *Memento*, about the guy with no short term memory who wakes up with amnesia every morning.

When we arrived at the frat house, two guys sat on the deck

smoking cigarettes.

"Hey Alex," one of them said.

"Hey," Alex said. "This is Jason. He lives down the hall from me in the dorms. Jason, this is Dan."

"Hey," I said. We shook hands.

"Nice to meet you," Dan said, promptly turning his attention back to Alex. "It's pretty lame in there."

"Yeah?"

"Yeah. I mean, it's okay, but we can't drink in the house. There's going to be an after party though," Dan said, and his face lit up. "We'll head over there in like an hour. Don't worry. You guys will have a fun night."

"I'll come find you after we're done in here," Alex said, and he walked through the front door.

We walked into a wide, open space. The bare floorboards creaked as we walked over them. The house looked like a piece of shit. I felt like a government official might pop up at any moment and condemn it. For some reason, I really liked the atmosphere afforded by such a house. It felt gritty—the kind of party house I'd seen in movies. The only difference was that, apparently, there was no drinking in this frat house. At least, not tonight.

Off to the right, there was a kitchen. Alex walked to the fridge. "You want something to drink?" he asked.

"Sure," I said. Maybe I'd misheard; maybe I *would* be able to drink here.

"Mountain Dew or Coke?" Alex asked as he leaned into the fridge.

"Um . . . Coke, I guess."

"Let's see what's going on upstairs," Alex said as he handed me an ice-cold can.

We walked up the stairs and when we reached the second

## Part II: Marijuana

floor I saw a balcony snaking across the perimeter, overlooking the lower level, so people could look down at the people partying below.

"This is kind of cool," I said.

"Yeah, it is," he agreed.

A pair of attractive girls, both blondes, leaned over the rail engaged in conversation.

"Hello ladies," Alex said.

They didn't look up.

"Let's go check out the bedrooms," he said.

He led me down a narrow hallway with doors on either side—the frat members' bedrooms, I realized.

"I really like it here," Alex said. "All the guys are really cool. I've had trouble making friends since I came here, but these guys accept me for who I am. I'm thinking about pledging next year."

I was surprised to hear these words coming from Alex. He sounded like *me*, with his talk about how hard it was to make friends. Hadn't he made friends with Joel (before he'd fucked it up by sleeping with his girlfriend?) But come to think of it, I couldn't think of any other friends Alex had except for Joel and me. If it was hard for a bold guy like Alex to make friends, maybe it was understandable that it was hard for me.

"That would be cool," I said. "Maybe I'll pledge."

"Yeah, dude. You totally should."

We headed downstairs and watched some of the frat guys play pool and make asses out of themselves. Just when I thought I couldn't take any more jokes about sticking pool cues up each other's asses, Alex grabbed my arm.

"Let's find Dan and have him take us to the after party," he said.

"Finally!"

We walked uphill about five blocks and came to a one-story house, much smaller than the frat house.

"Come on in," Dan said. He burst through the door without knocking.

Besides four or five people wandering between the kitchen and the living room, we were the only people there. There was no alcohol to be seen.

"Sammy's coming with beer," Dan said as if he'd read my mind. "Sit tight. Make yourselves at home."

I sat down on the couch and Alex sat down on a chair facing me.

"So," I said.

"So," Alex said.

Awkward silence.

"Alex, come over here. There's someone I want you to meet," Dan said. Alex eagerly hopped off his chair and followed Dan into the kitchen, leaving me on the couch by myself.

I sat there feeling incredibly awkward, knowing that if anyone walked in I would instantly be pegged as a loser and shunned by everyone at the party, except for Alex, who would only acknowledge me out of pity.

The front door swung open and a heavyset man carrying two large cases of Budweiser walked in.

"You must be Sammy," I said.

He gave me a perplexed look.

"Yeah. I'm Sammy."

"Dan told us you were coming," I said, offering an awkward smile.

Sammy nodded, and then proceeded to completely ignore me as he continued on to the kitchen. I followed behind him so I could grab a beer.

## Part II: Marijuana

I popped off the lid and let the beer slide down my throat. It made me grimace, but I'd started to get somewhat used to the taste.

More people trickled in, but if anything, that made me feel even more uncomfortable. Everyone knew somebody else; everyone had someone they could talk to, except for me, sitting in the corner by myself. I got up and looked for Alex.

When I found him, he was talking to one of his buddies. He had a beer bottle in his hand, already mostly empty.

"Hey," I said, sidling up next to him.

"Jason!" Alex shouted, raising his hands high in the air.

"Uh . . . yeah. That's me."

"Come here," he said, and he gave me a bear hug.

"Good to see you too," I said uncomfortably. "I mean, what has it been . . . five minutes?"

"Worst five minutes of my life, apart from you," he said.

He was clearly already very, very wasted. This must not have been his first beer, I realized.

"Wow," I said. "I think I need to have a couple more beers to catch up to you."

"YES," he said intently. "Yes. You. Do. Get out of here. Drink, Jason. DRINK."

I walked back to the kitchen, chuckling to myself.

After a couple more beers, I felt the effects of the alcohol a lot more intensely, and was acting silly and probably making a fool of myself. But Alex and I were having a good time. I was glad. It seemed I was solidifying a budding friendship. Even though Alex had a tendency to annoy me and come across as a little needy, we genuinely had a good time together that night.

"Hey guys." Dan popped up from nowhere. "We're taking this party down to the basement. Let's go!"

I followed Dan and Alex down to the basement. Several people had already gathered there. In the center of the room were two very large hookahs sitting on top of a "table" that was actually just a sheet of plywood on top of two sawhorses. One of the hookahs only had two hoses, but the other had four.

I had never seen a hookah before, so I was startled to see the large hoses creeping out of them like the legs of some giant insect. I pointed to them and asked Alex under my breath so nobody else would hear me, "What are those things?"

He gave me a sideways glance. "You don't know what a hookah is?"

"I don't think so . . ."

"Haven't you ever seen *Alice in Wonderland*?"

"Yeah."

"Well that's what the caterpillar smokes out of when he blows smoke rings—a hookah."

"Oh."

"And now I am going to go take a hit off this thing and get really fucked up," he said.

"Fucked up?"

"Yeah. There's weed in these things, dude."

I was certainly feeling rather uninhibited from all the beer, but I was still wary of marijuana. I wasn't sure I'd liked the sensation when I'd smoked pot with Katie. Then again, I wasn't sure I'd liked the sensation the first time I'd had alcohol, and I'd come to enjoy that quite a bit. If marijuana could make me more social, I reasoned, maybe I ought to try it.

I stood next to Alex as he placed the end of the hose into his mouth, inhaled for a long time, and then exhaled a thick plume of white smoke.

He extended the end of the hose to me and looked at me expectantly.

## Part II: Marijuana

I stood watching his outstretched arm for what felt like a full minute, weighing the pros and cons of smoking marijuana. I had been so adamant about not doing it; it was against my moral convictions. But another part of me wanted to rebel against those moral convictions. The guys that drank and smoked pot were the guys getting laid, weren't they? They were the wild ones, the party animals, the bad boys, the fun guys women wanted inside them.

I wanted women to want me inside them.

"Jason?"

"Uh . . . No thanks, man."

I didn't want to get inside them this way, I finally decided. Alcohol was one thing. Marijuana was another. I wasn't ready to become a pothead.

"Suit yourself," Alex said just before he took another deep, long hit off the hookah.


My first summer back from school, I once again turned to the internet to make friends.

I met a girl online named Brianna. She managed to look cute and edgy at the same time in her online photograph. While her face was round and had soft features, she also had an eyebrow piercing and her hair was dyed black. She looked like a good girl trying to rebel a little.

It was around this time I decided to start smoking marijuana socially.

Granted, I hadn't actually done so yet. I still hadn't smoked pot since the night with Katie, but I'd been discouraged that drinking in and of itself hadn't won me legions of friends. I still hung out with Alex and Joel, but that was about it. I wasn't surrounded by hot, drunk college chicks every weekend, and I didn't know why. I thought back to the night Alex and I wound up in that basement with the hookahs. Maybe if I'd taken a hit, I would have loosened up enough to convince a girl to come back to my dorm with me.

I read an article on an online medical website warning that the combination of alcohol and marijuana really fucked you up (although it didn't use those exact words). That must be my solution, I decided. It wasn't enough to just get drunk. To really get nuts at parties, to really put myself out there and make friends, I had to get *crunk*.[*]

I gently broached the subject of marijuana with Brianna when we instant messaged each other.

OH YEAH, she typed. I LOVE GETTING HIGH!

SWEET, I typed back. YOU KNOW WHERE TO GET SOME?

OH YEAH. I HAVE CONNECTIONS.

WE SHOULD GET STONED TONIGHT, THEN!

SOUNDS LIKE A PLAN TO ME, DUDE!

She gave me her phone number and directions to her house and in an hour, after making a couple wrong turns, I pulled into her driveway.

She walked onto her porch to meet me. Disappointment washed over me. Her face was as cute as advertised, but she was clearly overweight. Not obese, but not what one would call "fit." She had just a few too many extra pounds.

"Hi," she said.

"Hey," I said. "I made it."

A petite redhead emerged from the house and stood beside her.

---

[*] According to one definition on Urbandictionary.com, the word "crunk" originates from "smoking chronic (marijuana) and getting drunk." Just in case that was too complicated a definition, it goes on to say: "Chronic + Drunk = CRUNK."

## Part II: Marijuana

"This is my friend Ashley," Brianna said.

"Hi Ashley."

Brianna scrunched her eyebrows.

"Uh . . . what was your name again, dude?"

"Jason." *Fantastic. I'm so forgettable, even this fat chick doesn't remember my name.* I can be a real dick in my head sometimes.

"Right, right. Ashley, this is Jason."

"Hi Jason," she said, and she held out her hand. I shook it gently, feeling a rush of blood to my penis as her soft skin brushed against mine.

"We have to smoke outside," Brianna said. "If my dad comes home and smells pot smoke in the house, he'll kill me."

"That's fine." It was a warm summer night, so I had absolutely no problem with smoking outside.

We stood on her porch and she produced a small glass pipe not unlike the one Katie had produced more than a year ago. She loaded the bowl, took a drag, and passed it on to Ashley. Ashley took a drag and passed it to me.

I struggled to light the bowl and suck in the smoke at the same time. My cheeks flushed with embarrassment.

"It's been awhile since I've smoked," I said. "I've only ever smoked pot once."

"Wow, really?" Brianna sounded surprised.

"Yeah."

"Why just the once?"

"I didn't really like it."

She shot me a raised eyebrow. "But you like it now?"

"Hey," I said with a shrug. "College does that to people."

Both the girls laughed.

"We wouldn't know," Brianna said. "I've never gone to college and Ashley . . ."

"And Ashley . . . ?" I parroted.

"I'm still in high school," she said sheepishly.

That startled me. Brianna was twenty. I'd assumed Ashley was around her age.

"How old are you?" I asked.

"Seventeen."

Dammit. I'd found myself immediately attracted to Ashley and the thought of having sex with her had definitely crossed my mind. Now I felt like a dirty old pervert.

"Nice," I said, not knowing what else to say. "Now help me light this fucking bowl."

I held the pipe up to my mouth and as I sucked, Brianna lit the bowl for me. I inhaled . . . and my throat instantly erupted in an uncontrollable coughing fit.

The girls laughed again, a sound I was getting used to . . . and that I liked.

"I told you it's been awhile," I said.

"That's good though," Brianna said. "When you cough, it gets you more high."

"Really?"

"Yeah."

A lot of misinformation gets passed around in the underground world of stoners, so I had no idea whether that was true or not. To this day, I'm not sure—why would coughing enhance the process of getting baked?* If anything I'd think coughing would inhibit the process.

I passed the bowl back to Brianna and she took a hit. When

---

* According to a quick online search, the theory is that when you cough, your lungs expand, and that exposes more of your lungs' surface area to the THC in the smoke. But, from what I can tell, there's no scientific consensus on the matter, so that may or may not be true.

## Part II: Marijuana

the pipe came back to me, I tried to light it myself and managed, just barely, to take a successful hit.

"How are you feeling?" Ashley asked.

"I'm not really feeling it," I said. My coughing fit cut the first hit short, and I wasn't sure I'd lit the bowl properly the second time around. But Brianna was convinced I just needed a little time for it to kick in. She produced a pack of cigarettes from her pocket.

"Here," she said, handing me a cigarette.

"I don't smoke," I said.

"Listen to yourself. You've been smoking for the past five minutes."

"Yeah, but tobacco's bad for you."

"It's not like you're going to get addicted off one drag. The nicotine gets you higher, quicker.[†] Take a puff or two and I'll finish it off for you."

"Fine," I said. I lit the cigarette with no problem, brought the filtered end to my mouth, and breathed the smoke into my lungs. It soared down my throat a lot smoother than the marijuana smoke had.

"Not bad," I said after exhaling a wispy trail of smoke. I took another drag then handed the cigarette back to Brianna.

We passed the pipe around a few more times until Brianna declared it spent. We went back inside. Brianna, who had been texting off and on while we smoked, announced she wanted to pick up a guy from a local military base.

"Is he a good friend of yours?" I asked.

"No. I've talked to him online. This would be my first time meeting him in person . . . like you."

---

† I have no idea whether or not this is true.

Shit. How was I going to compete with a military guy? I was boring enough without having some cocky, fit, macho Army dude come into play, making me look like a wuss. But I wasn't about to protest—I didn't want to seem as insecure as I felt.

"Let's go," I said. "Road trip." I crawled into the back seat of Brianna's little two-door sedan, and we were off.

Brianna turned on her radio and while we drove, the marijuana hit me. My blood buzzed and the slow-motion sensation returned. I closed my eyes and listened to the music. Vibrant colors swirled about, dancing in time to the sound.

I was really, really stoned. And I enjoyed it.

When we drove into the Army base (was it really a good idea to drive stoned onto an Army base, I wondered?) Brianna called the guy—his name was Mike—and he seemed to spring up out of nowhere just before he jumped into the backseat next to me.

"Hey, man," he said.

"Hi," I said. I looked him over judgingly. He *was* fit, but he wasn't a huge muscle man or anything. He had a buzz cut, and he had horrible, horrible acne all over his face and neck. Each bright red pimple was the size of a dime, inflamed and irritated. It was disgusting.

He was perfect.

"Look what I got," he said. He held up a brown paper bag. Apparently, he'd gone to the liquor store and spent a hundred bucks on booze.

The girls chirped excitedly, but then the car became a prison of awkwardness. We made idle chit-chat here and there, but it suddenly dawned on us that none of us really knew each other (except for Brianna and Ashley, of course—but even then, I wasn't sure they knew each other all that well).

When we got back to Brianna's house, we gratefully climbed

## Part II: Marijuana

out of the car and hurried into the house. I excused myself to the restroom and when I came back Mike had set up all his booze bottles on the kitchen counter. Brianna and Ashley helped themselves to shots of rum.

I looked over the bottles and gave an approving nod.

"Patron . . . I've heard of this. Isn't it expensive?"

"Yeah," Mike said proudly. "This little bottle was almost fifty bucks all by itself! But it goes down smooth. It's worth it."

"I have to try some of this," I said. I uncorked the bottle and leaned it over the mouth of a shot glass. "I've heard how good this stuff is, but I've never been able to afford it."

"Help yourself, man," Mike said. "We're all here to have a good time."

I wasn't asking his permission, but whatever.

I tipped the shot glass into my mouth and let the tequila burn its way down my throat. I grimaced. It was still alcohol. It still packed an uncomfortable punch—it wasn't Mike's Hard Lemonade—but it *did* go down smooth, relatively speaking. And it had kind of a nice flavor to it.

I poured myself another shot.

After about my third shot, Mike and I walked into Brianna's bedroom. The girls sat on the bed watching *Dude, Where's My Car?* Mike hopped on to the bed beside them. It pissed me off because the bed was only wide enough for three people. I took a seat on the floor by the foot of the bed.

"You sure you don't want to sit up here?" Brianna asked. "We can make room."

"No, no," I said. "It'll be too uncomfortable if we're all squeezed together. I don't mind sitting here." I *did* mind, but I wasn't about to admit it. Brianna shrugged and everyone's attention turned to the TV screen.

"Have you guys seen this movie?" Brianna asked.

"It's one of my favorites," Mike said.

"It's a good one," I said demurely. In fact, I thought it was a mediocre movie at best. A few laughs, but overall, pretty stupid. But I didn't want to stick out. I didn't want these people to think I was some kind of stuck-up snoot, although in some ways I was—compared to them, anyway. That didn't mean I couldn't enjoy a good stoner movie, considering I was quite baked and well on my way to becoming drunk as well.

We laughed as the movie progressed, but about halfway through we grew tired. The laughter subsided and we watched the movie in silence. I looked over my shoulder at one point and saw that Ashley was now sitting with her back against Mike's chest. A shiver of jealousy shot through me. Who the fuck did this guy think he was?

But I chided myself. This girl was *seventeen*. I shouldn't be interested in her anyway. Not unless I wanted jail time.

But Mike was twenty-four. Did he think he could get away with fucking this girl? If so, why couldn't I? She'd probably already slept with dozens of guys twice her age. Why couldn't I add my name to the list?

*Yeah, and catch one of the myriad diseases those dozens of guys have given her. Leave it alone, Jason.*

I tried to. But I was still jealous. As I watched the movie, I stewed in anger.

Apparently their sensual cuddling was affecting Brianna, too, because she got up without a word and walked out. Ashley's women's intuition sensed something was amiss, and she went after her, leaving Mike and I alone, awkwardly watching Ashton Kutcher and Seann William Scott together.

I made out snippets of the girls' conversation. Ashley

## Part II: Marijuana

demanded Brianna tell her what was wrong. Brianna denied there was anything wrong, but the tone of her voice made it apparent something was. It made me feel even more like shit. Clearly Brianna wanted Mike spooning with *her*, not Ashley, which meant I was the odd fucking duck out. Nobody wanted me. What was I doing, wasting my time here?

Ashley returned and resumed her spooning position with Mike. After a few minutes I turned around and saw Mike's hands running up and down Ashley's sides, under her shirt. Their breath was heavy. Ashley's eyes were closed. Her hips bucked slightly with every downward stroke of Mike's hands.

I left so they could be alone.

I went to the bathroom to take a piss and then went to find Brianna. I found her outside on the porch smoking a cigarette. I was surprised it was already starting to get light outside. I checked the time on my cell phone. It was four in the morning.

"Hey," I said.

"Hey. Sorry this has been so awkward."

"It hasn't been that awkward," I lied. "I had fun."

"Really?"

"Yeah." *Hell no.*

"I'm sorry about Ashley. She can be such a fucking slut sometimes."

"Yes, well, can't we all?" I said with a laugh. Brianna chuckled sympathetically. "I'm going to go," I said.

"Are you sure you're okay to drive?"

"I'm pretty sure," I said. The pot and alcohol had mostly worn off. I felt sober, just very, very tired.

"Alright. It was nice meeting you," Brianna said. She opened her arms wide for a hug. We embraced briefly and awkwardly and I gave a backwards wave as I walked to my car.

On my way home, I stopped at a red light. There was a car behind me. The left turn lane had a green arrow. All of a sudden the car roared around me and turned left at the empty intersection.

*What an asshole*, I thought. *If he forgot to get in the turn lane, he should have backed up and gotten into it instead of going around me like that.*

Then I looked around and realized *I* was in the turn lane. *I* was the asshole.

Maybe the pot *hadn't* worn off completely.

Joel stayed with his dad that summer. His dad happened to live a little less than an hour away from my parent's house. He invited me to visit him there on the weekend. For some reason, I decided I needed to impress him by coming with marijuana.

The trouble was, I didn't know where to get any.

When I texted Brianna to find out where she got hers, she gave me Ashley's phone number.

I called Ashley and told her that Brianna said she could help me get some pot.

"Yeah, I could probably do that," she said. "Let me call someone and I'll see if he's available."

"Oh, you mean . . . right now?"

"Yeah. I'll call you back in a sec."

She called back in a few minutes.

"You know where the Shari's is off Main?"

"Yeah."

"Meet me there in half an hour. How much did you want?"

"Um . . . how much will twenty bucks get me?"

"About two grams."

"That sounds good." I had no idea if that was fair or not, but

## Part II: Marijuana

I wasn't in a position to nitpick.

"See you soon."

"Bye."

I pulled into Shari's and scanned the parking lot for Ashley. I didn't know what kind of car she drove. I didn't see her so I pulled into the most isolated parking space I could find and waited.

She showed up ten minutes late and parked in the space next to mine. I wadded my cash into a ball and palmed it. I stepped out of my car and opened the passenger-side door of her car.

"Come in," she said.

I took a seat in the car, feeling nervous as I did so.

"You have the money?" she asked. I was reminded of my experience with the prostitute. I was getting into all sorts of shady business.

"Yeah," I said. "I have it right here." I revealed the wad of money concealed in my palm. She took it from my hand and withdrew a plastic baggie of marijuana from her jacket pocket. She handed it to me. I was a bit upset at how business-like this whole thing seemed. We had hung out the other night like friends, and even though the night had taken an awkward turn, it made me feel like shit to be treated like just another drug dealer's customer. In hindsight, as a seventeen-year-old drug dealer, she was probably just as nervous as I was.

I grabbed the door handle and prepared to turn it, but Ashley stopped me.

"Don't leave yet," she said. "Sit and chill for a minute." I must have looked at her oddly, because after a moment she added, "We don't want this to look like a drug deal."

As we sat there awkwardly, not saying a word to each other, I thought we must look a lot more conspicuous than we would have if I had just left promptly.

"Okay," she said after a few minutes. "You can go now." By the tone of her voice it sounded like I was inconveniencing her or something.

"Thanks a lot," I said, not really meaning it. "I appreciate it. See you later."

I never saw her again.

I GOT LOST on the way to Joel's dad's house. The directions I'd gotten off the internet were wrong and Joel had only given me vague directions—he didn't know the name of a single street. His dad's house was in the middle of the woods so I got spotty phone service and couldn't call for directions, or even to tell him I was going to be late. Two hours after leaving my house, I finally found his dad's place.

It was more of a trailer than a house—a nice, big trailer, but not the kind of home I'd been expecting. I parked on the street and Joel came out onto the porch to greet me.

"Hey," I said. "Sorry I'm late. I got lost."

"I thought I gave you pretty straightforward directions," he said in a subtly accusing tone.

*Are you fucking kidding me?* I thought. *You gave me the worst fucking directions in the world. You might as well have just said, "Drive for an hour, take some turns, and you'll end up at my house eventually."*

Instead of saying that, I tried to defuse the tension I felt with some self-deprecating humor. "I have a terrible sense of direction," I said with a chuckle. "I'm always getting lost."

Joel shrugged. He ushered me through the front door and introduced me to his dad and his dad's girlfriend.

His dad looked more or less like an older version of Joel. He

## Part II: Marijuana

was a couple inches taller than him, balding, and had a short but full beard. His dad's girlfriend was a little on the chubby side and looked a couple years older than him. Her hair was already graying, whereas his—what was left of it, anyway—was still dark, assuming he didn't color it. They were both nice and friendly and made small-talk with me, asking me what I was going to school for and all the other requisite "get-to-know-you" questions.

After a few moments they sensed that Joel and I wanted to hang out by ourselves, so they excused themselves and left us alone in the living room.

"So," I said. "I brought some pot."

"Oh, yeah?" Joel said. "Let me see it."

"Here? Right now?" I looked over my shoulder to see if his dad was within earshot.

"They don't give a shit," he said. "They both smoke pot."

"They do?"

"Yeah. I mean, not all the time or anything. Every once in a while."

"Oh," I said. "Okay." I dug the baggie out of my pocket and handed it to Joel.

"How much did you pay for this?" he asked.

"Twenty bucks."

"Looks about right."

"Really? I was afraid I might have gotten ripped off."

"I'm not an expert or anything, but I don't think you got ripped off. If you did, not by much."

"Awesome. Okay. Well. Should we smoke it?"

"Hell yeah." He got a pipe, loaded a bowl, and passed it to me. I lit the bowl and took a deep, long hit. I was getting used to this now. I could light the bowl by myself and I felt myself getting high after just one or two hits instead of four or five. I handed the pipe back to Joel. He took a drag. We cracked jokes, laughed, and had a good time even though we weren't really doing anything or talking about anything substantive.

When I left for home, I thought I had sobered up enough to drive. But I realized after a few minutes on the road that my eyes still had that sensation of moving in slow motion in their sockets. *Crap*, I thought. *I'd better drive extra carefully.*

When I arrived at my parent's house my brother was in the living room. He'd rented a small house with a friend of his, but he was home all the time eating our parent's food and using the washing machine, i.e., our mom.

He and his roommate were having a party next weekend, he announced.

"I need you to pick up the keg," he said.

"You got a keg?"

He laughed. "Yeah. Don't worry, it's all paid for and everything, we just need you to pick it up since you're the only one over twenty-one."

A year ago, I would have refused. I would have given him a lengthy lecture about how it was irresponsible for underage kids to drink and have big, wild parties.

But that was last year. This was now.

"Sure," I said.

# The Party

> One should know that Nature is illusion *maya*, and that Brahman is the illusion maker. This whole world is pervaded with beings that are part of him.
> —Svetasvatara Unapnishad

The next Saturday I picked up the keg and tap from the bar and drove it back to my brother's house. He walked out of the house with his arms in the air when I arrived.

"Now the party can begin!" he said.

There were only five people there. My brother had filled a large garbage can with ice. We each grabbed one side of the keg and lowered it in.

I had invited Joel and his girlfriend, Mary, to come, but they wouldn't be arriving until later. In the meantime, it was just me, my brother Tim, his girlfriend Lisa, my brother's roommate,

Cole, and his friend Aaron.

It was a hot summer day. We sat in lawn chairs just outside the door. My brother passed a bong to Aaron.

"Let me get a hit off that," I said.

Tim's eyebrows leapt up in surprise.

"I didn't know you smoked."

"I just started recently. I've never smoked out of one of these things before, though."

"Oh yeah?" he asked with a laugh. "You've never smoked out of a bong, huh?"

"Yeah. A . . . bong." I'd seen bongs in movies, but I didn't know what they were called.

"Well here, have a blast," he said, handing it to me.

I walked it to a lawn chair and lodged it between my thighs as I had seen the others do.

"Okay. Now what?"

"Hold on," he said. "Let me show you how it's done." He retrieved his drug apparatus and took it back to his chair.

"This, here, is where you inhale the smoke from," he said, pointing to the mouthpiece. "You place your lips around it and light the weed in this little bowl here," he said, pointing to it. "Then, after the smoke builds up, you withdraw the stem, inhale the smoke, hold it in, and blow it out. Watch."

I watched intently as he went through the process. Even though I was a complete novice, I didn't want to look like one in front of my younger brother.

"There," he said after exhaling. "You try it."

He handed me the bong. I cradled it like a baby and placed it carefully between my legs. Tim handed me a lighter and I went over all the steps just to make sure I understood correctly.

I placed my lips over the mouthpiece. I lit the bowl. I removed

## The Party

the stem. I sucked in the smoke. I held it in. I blew it out.

The marijuana hit my head like a sledgehammer.

"Holy crap," I said. "That's way better than a pipe."

Everyone laughed. I took another hit.

"That feels amazing," I said. "I'm going inside to get myself a beer."

I walked inside, grabbed a plastic cup, and filled it with beer from the keg. I came back outside and downed my beer within a minute or two. I may have been a novice when it came to smoking pot, but when it came to drinking beer I was practically a seasoned veteran.

I went back inside for more.

When I came back outside, I joined the conversation that my brother was having with his friends. They laughed, I laughed; we all had a good time.

*This is what I've longed for*, I thought to myself. *Sitting back, relaxing, having a good time. Not constantly worrying about what people think of me. Not over-analyzing every word out of my mouth. Just being myself.*

I credited the combination of weed and beer with the erasure of my anxiety.

Getting crunk *worked*.

The house Tim was living in at the time had a big yard. He had set up a fire pit in the middle of it for a big bonfire. But it was the middle of summer and everything was dry and crisp and susceptible to catching fire. I was concerned.

"What precautions are you taking in case there's a fire?" I asked.

"None," he said nonchalantly

"That's no good at all!" I yelled. I grabbed the end of the hose from the side of the house and ran it into the field, unspooling the hose as I went. Tim immediately jumped up and grabbed the hose.

"No, Jason," he said, half-jokingly. He was clearly pretty crunk himself. "It's not necessary."

"Yes it is!" I shouted, way too loudly. My inhibitions had completely dissolved. Suddenly, we were engaged in a very bizarre tug-of-war, battling for control of the hose until we both fell to the ground, shaking with laughter.

Later that night, Joel and his girlfriend Mary showed up to the party.

"Joel!" I shouted far too enthusiastically. I gave him a hug that lasted a little too long. "Joel! This is my brother!" I said, gesturing toward Tim.

Joel gave my brother a knowing look.

"He's drunk," he said pointing to me.

"And stoned," my brother added.

"I'm not *that* fucked up," I said.

Everyone looked at me skeptically.

"Okay," I said. "I'm pretty fucked up."

The night after that point gets pretty hazy. Joel tried to record me saying inappropriate things on his cell phone, but when he asked me to repeat them I got wise and kept my mouth shut.

At some point I nearly passed out and used a girl's lap as a pillow. Thankfully, she seemed amused and not annoyed. These were experiences I would never have dreamed of having sober, chained by my inhibitions. Alcohol and marijuana were freeing.

The next morning, my brother and his girlfriend made waffles for everyone that had stayed the night. I was extremely hungover, but I didn't care. I felt more free and liberated with this pounding

## The Party

headache than I'd ever felt sober, when I'd been wracked by anxiety.

But I was entering dangerous territory. I was arguably beginning to enjoy drugs and alcohol too much. I used them as a crutch. I still couldn't socialize with people sober. Substance abuse was not a permanent solution, but I was treating it like one.

And although I didn't realize it at the time, the lifestyle I'd adopted was leading me straight into salvia's waiting arms.

# Salvia

I do not exist. Only you exist.
—MEWITHOUTYOU, "In a Sweater Poorly Knit"

I didn't have a summer job, so I didn't have any money. When Katie invited me to a birthday party her friends were throwing for her, my mind immediately went into overdrive, plotting a way to acquire a birthday present.

"You don't need to get a gift," she said immediately, sensing my anxiety.

That made me feel a little better—not because I wasn't going to get a gift; I *had* to get one. But when she opened up my gift and saw that it was cheap and crappy, it would look better than no gift at all.

Almost a year earlier, I had borrowed a copy of Philip Pullman's *The Golden Compass* from her. I decided to wrap up her book and give it back to her. As long as I told her before she opened it that it was a "joke gift," I figured it would make her laugh and thus make up, to some degree, for the fact that it wasn't a real gift.

Unfortunately, I couldn't find the copy she had lent me.

I went to a used bookstore. Luckily, they had a copy, so I bought it, threw it in a gift bag with some tissue paper, and drove to the party.

I parked on the street and texted Katie as I walked to the house to let her know I was there. She called me.

"Where are you now?"

"I'm walking up the driveway now . . . up the steps . . . at the door . . ."

The door swung open and there was Katie, standing in the doorway with two other girls standing beside her.

"Hi!"

"Hi!" I said, closing my phone. "Happy birthday!"

"Thank you!" she said. We hugged. When we parted, I handed her the gift bag with *The Golden Compass* in it.

"This is for you," I said. "It's kind of a joke, so don't get your hopes up."

"Didn't I tell you not to get me a gift?"

"Well, technically I didn't. Just open it and see."

Intrigued, she walked into the living room with the bag and I followed her. She sat down on the couch and tore through the tissue paper.

She laughed.

"You gave me my book back!"

"Yeah," I said. "Only it's not the same edition. I couldn't find the copy you lent me, so I bought another copy at a used bookstore."

"It's great, Jason. I love it. I wanted to reread it before the movie came out."

"You're welcome," I said.

"Do you want some beer or something?" she asked. "There's lots of beer in the fridge, and lots of liquor in the kitchen."

"Sure, I guess," I said. *Of course I want some free booze*, I thought. "Just help myself?"

"Yep," she said.

I walked into the kitchen and my mouth watered involuntarily as I took in the countertop, filled with at least a dozen liquor bottles, all representing a variety of different spirits.

"Jackpot," I whispered to myself.

Shot glasses lined the counter—most of them looked like souvenirs from various vacation destinations. I grabbed one of the cleaner-looking ones and poured myself a shot of whiskey. I downed it, then looked through the rest of the liquor.

My eyes turned to a bottle of Goldschläger—the Italian peppermint schnapps with gold flakes in it. The urban myth is that the gold flakes form tiny cuts after the liquor's ingested, allowing the alcohol to enter the bloodstream directly and intoxicate the drinker more quickly. I've since found out that's not true, but I didn't know that at the time and was intrigued by the concept. I poured myself a shot, downed it, and decided that was enough liquor. It was time to turn to beer. I grabbed one out of the fridge and wandered out onto the deck, where everyone had congregated.

A boombox sitting on the windowsill blasted some intolerable gangster rap, but with the alcohol I'd ingested taking effect, I didn't mind. I tapped my foot as I sipped my beer and studied my fellow partygoers.

Most of them seemed preppy, as if they'd walked out of an

Abercrombie and Fitch catalogue. Not exactly my style. At that time in my life I'd spent most of my energy—not entirely successfully—trying to fit in with the alternative crowd. But it was a party, and there was free booze, so there was no reason I couldn't hang with this crowd for the night.

As I scanned the deck, I caught sight of two shadowy forms writhing on a bench in the corner. They were clearly making out and a grin spread across my face. *My kind of party.*

They shifted slightly, into the light, and I saw that they were both men.

*Okay. Definitely* not *my kind of party.*

I turned around and went to go find Katie. I found her in the kitchen pouring herself a shot.

"There's two guys making out on the deck," I said with a nervous laugh.

"Oh yeah," she said. "Everyone here is gay."

"Everyone?"

"Well, almost everyone." She swung back her head and emptied her shot glass. "There's maybe three or four straight people here. And I think one or two might be bisexual."

"So not a good chance of picking up any girls, then?" I joked.

"Not likely. But that doesn't mean you can't have fun! Come on." She led me back to the deck. We stood there awkwardly for a moment.

"Are you going to introduce me to anyone?" I asked.

"Oh, I hardly know anyone here."

"What?"

"They're Grant's friends." Grant was a friend of hers she'd lived with briefly a year earlier. He was bisexual.

The party was starting to make sense.

I downed the rest of my beer and went in to get a new one.

I didn't know anyone there. I figured I might as well get drunk and make myself sociable.

When I came back out I surveyed the deck. It was chaos, a cacophony of people running around, dancing and smoking weed out of bongs and pipes. Katie had given up weed, but when I pointed out the bong to her, her eyes sparkled a little. But she shook her head. "I don't do that anymore," she said.

Our roles had reversed. I was the drug-fueled partier, while responsibility had wound its way around Katie like a boa constrictor. Even so, she wasn't a complete teetotaler—she still drank alcohol. And she was underage.

A patio table sat at the center of the deck, littered with shot glasses, beer cans and plastic cups. A box sat on the corner of the table. I walked over and picked it up, studying it curiously.

"What's this?"

"It's Jenga." I'd expected Katie to answer, but it was a feminine yet slightly husky voice that met my ears instead. I looked around and saw that Katie had migrated to the opposite side of the deck to chat with Grant. Standing beside me was a slender, dark-skinned woman. Her hair was trimmed short and a permanent smile—almost a sneer—sat delicately on her face.

"Jenga?"

"Yeah," she said. "Jenga. You know, the game where you pile up the blocks, and then take turns removing them one by one. The person who makes it all collapse loses."

"Oh, right. Jenga."

"But this," she said, and her smile grew, "is the drinking version of the game."

"The drinking version? I didn't know such a thing existed."

"Look." She opened the box and removed one of the wooden blocks. It said, "Remove one piece of clothing."

I laughed. "I see. So it's like strip poker . . . but with Jenga."

"No, they're all different. Look." She dropped a handful of blocks into my arms. Several fell onto the floor. I lowered the blocks in my arms to the tabletop and sorted through them. They said things like, "do an impression," "take a shot," and "beer bitch."

"You have to do whatever the block you pull says."

"So what does this one mean," I said, pointing to the block that said "beer bitch."

"That means you're the beer bitch for the night—you have to get everyone's drinks."

*I could use a beer bitch.* "Let's play it!" I yelled.

She seemed just as enthusiastic. She gathered everyone around the table and stacked the blocks up carefully. She started us off by carefully pulling out a block.

Five more people took their turns pulling blocks, laughing when they read the ridiculous task assigned to them.

Finally, it was my turn.

I pinched the end of a block between my thumb and forefinger and, as gently as I could, pulled it out.

"Kiss the person to your left," I read aloud.

I turned to my left and the dark-skinned, short-haired chick gave me a mischievous grin. I suddenly grew bashful.

I leaned in to kiss her on the cheek, but she darted in and pressed her lips against mine. As our lips parted, I giggled nervously and blushed.

"Sorry," she said. "I didn't think it was a big deal. I'm gay."

"No problem," I said. I turned away shyly.

It only took a few more turns for someone to pull a block and send the tower tumbling down, spewing blocks all over. I didn't get another turn. I suppose that was to be expected; by its very nature, drunken Jenga couldn't last *that* long.

## Salvia

I ran into the kitchen to grab another beer. I had gotten quite drunk, and my inhibitions were as totally and devastatingly smashed as I was. I had no problem talking to every person that passed by. It was what I wanted every day to be like.

I walked back to the deck and looked around. A long-haired boy who looked like a hippie straight out of the seventies sat in the corner taking a hit off a glass pipe.

"Hey," I said, "are you smoking weed?"

"Yeah," he said, surprised to see someone he'd never met talking to him. "You want a hit?"

"Well," I said with a smile, "just a little one."

He handed me his pipe and a small butane lighter. I took a hit and laughed after I exhaled the smoke.

"That felt nice," I said. "Mind if I take another hit?"

"Help yourself," he said. He sounded genuinely cheerful about it. Not stingy at all.

I took another hit and after I exhaled I handed the pipe back to him.

"Thanks, man," I said.

"No problem."

Normally I would have left it at that, but I was getting incredibly inebriated and I felt comfortable talking further.

"Do you know Katie?" I asked.

"Yeah," he said. "We used to hang out all the time."

"Nice. I guess she doesn't know a lot of people here."

"I know. Isn't that weird? Going to a birthday party where most of the guests don't even know who you are?"

"In a way, I think it's kind of fun. You get to make new friends."

He pointed his finger at me. "That, my friend, is exactly right."

"I'm Jason, by the way," I said and I held out my hand. He

gripped it and shook vigorously.

"I'm Colin," he said. "Nice to meet you."

"You too."

We stood there a moment. I took a sip of my beer and he took a hit off his pipe.

"I'll catch you later, Colin."

"See you later, Jason."

I walked around the deck, looking for new friends. I talked to several people, but I was so buzzed by that point, and the conversations were so frivolous, I can't remember what any of them were about.

The alcohol and marijuana waltzed together in my brain, stepping on my pleasure centers and plastering a grin on my face. I felt relaxed and happy, bordering on giddy, and it seemed life couldn't get any better. My life finally seemed headed in the right direction. I was finally able to talk to people and form relationships. So what if I needed drugs and alcohol to do so? If it worked, it worked.

That's when the short-haired, dark-skinned girl—my Jenga princess—mentioned salvia.

*There's a tingling sensation in my right thigh. It seems inconsequential at first. It's the same sensation I get when my leg falls asleep. But suddenly the sensation isn't isolated to my thigh. It travels up my side, up my right arm, and into my brain. There's a weird sensation in my head now that I can't quite put my finger on.*

*Now there's a spinning sensation. Everything drags down and to the right. It's not just me—the entire universe is being pulled into a vortex in the corner of some impossibly gargantuan room. Down and to the right, down and to the right, inevitably, irrevocably, and as much as I try to resist it, the pull is unavoidable.*

# Salvia

*As the spinning and pulling continue, my perspective shifts and I'm riding along several layers of reality that are rapidly peeling away, one right after the other as if someone's peeling off a potato's skin, except once they peel off one layer of skin, there's another beneath it, so they repeat the process again and again. Each layer is a level of illusion. Each layer has been carefully placed on top of the other to conceal the true nature of reality. Each layer is a deception, a dream, a mask. A little more truth is revealed with each one's removal. The truth becomes clearer and as it does I grow more and more apprehensive.*

*I look to my left at a wood picket fence surrounding the perimeter of the yard and suddenly a group of construction workers appears from nowhere and easily lifts the fence as if it were merely a prop in a movie, as if they've been asked to come dismantle the set. They walk off, laughing, and I realize everyone around me is giggling—giggling at me, amused by my concern, amused by how well they've tricked me into thinking this facade I called reality actually existed.*

*"What's happening?" I ask. The dark-skinned girl, hearing the concern in my voice, grabs my shoulders and says, "It's okay. You're tripping on salvia." But the words—both hers and mine—repeat, over and over again, becoming a rhythmic, ever-escalating call and response, as if the original exchange is echoing into eternity:*

> Wh—what's happening?
> Dude! You're tripping on salvia!
> Wh—what's happening?!
> *Dude!* You're tripping on *salvia!*
> Wh—what's *HAPPENING?!*
> *DUDE!* You're tripping on *SALVIA!*

*That chorus reverberates throughout the entire trip and suddenly it's not the dark-skinned girl saying it, it's some unearthly presence.*

*I can't tell if it's a woman or some genderless, entirely inhuman creature.*

Yet there's a familiarity to her, to all of this, as if I've experienced this exact scenario millions of times before. No, not millions—that figure is woefully inadequate.

The layers peeling away are no longer layers of reality. Now every removed layer represents time—a lifetime. A small piece of my ego peels away with each layer. I try to grasp these fleeing fragments of my essence, but they slide through my mental fingers and I realize it's hopeless. My self slowly fades and even though I am still somehow aware, it is without the benefit of an ego.

Every layer peeled away is now somebody's life and as it peels away, I live the life as if it were my own. It's like the motion of the layer being pulled away drags time along, like a flip book mimicking motion.

At first, I think it's cool I'm living other people's lives. But as soon as one life finishes another begins. By the millionth life, it is unbearable. Even as I live these lives, I am outside of them, unable to influence them. I am a hopeless, powerless spectator. Will this never end? What have I done? I've doomed myself to an eternity of living out futile, meaningless, insignificant lives.

Then I live every life at once, experiencing every possible moment, concentrated into a single, timeless instant. The sensation is overwhelming, painful, impossible.

Slowly, mercifully, the sensation fades.

Other images flash in my mind, images from my life. I see myself making love to Veronica. Another image, one I'm pretty sure I haven't actually lived, follows it. I'm on a stage, playing a guitar. I throw my instrument into the crowd, followed by my own body. I surf atop the crowd, but suddenly I'm somewhere else. The voice of an announcer calls, but I'm not sure what he's saying. *SALVIA* flashes in front of my eyes in big gold letters, like they've been plucked off the marquee of an old-timey theater, and as the letters pass before my eyes the announcer reads the word out loud as if he were shouting, "Let's get ready to rumble!"

Suddenly it all makes sense. I always thought my life was significant, that God existed and had a purpose for me. But salvia reveals to me that our lives are completely and utterly insignificant and not one of us is alive.

As my life unwinds and comes to a close, I see what the purpose of this universe is. The universe, which I'd been a part of, was nothing more than a yellow pixel doing its part to make up the logo of the television show Family Matters. That's all the universe is—a yellow pixel on somebody's cosmic television screen.

As the Family Matters theme finishes playing and the logo fades from the screen, the woman returns and explains that there indeed is no God and my whole life has been a lie, a façade, a joke. I vow to tell the world about this when I return and she laughs. Nobody will believe you, she explains. How do you know? I ask. Because this has been happening for eons, she replies. This journey is antediluvian, as old as anything in or outside of the universe.

I go back to living more lives, living each one in real time. Eons pass. Each lifetime is excruciating. Why won't this end? I'm weeping in my head. What have I done? What if I never come out of this trip? Of course I'll never come out of it. I've been dead for eons.

But suddenly the spiral gets brighter. There's a glimmer of hope. I feel like I'm getting closer to reality, closer to home. But it's taking so long. The wait is unbearable.

Then, in an instant, I'm back.

"*Holy shit!*" I fell onto my side. I didn't even put my hands up to cushion the fall. I just flopped over. It didn't hurt. The physical world still seemed distant after the metaphysical journey I'd just taken.

"Holy—Holy shit! *Holy shit! HOLY SHIT!*" I wasn't saying the words so much as half gasping, half screaming them.

"What happened?" someone asked.

"Holy shit!" I couldn't stop saying that! It's like my brain was a stuck record, playing the same few seconds of audio over and over. I just couldn't wrap my mind around what had just happened. It was so much more intense than I'd anticipated, not what I'd been expecting at all. "Holy shit" seemed like the only thing *to* say.

"Jason! What happened?"

"I—I lived a million lives! Holy shit! Holy *shit*! I lived a million lifetimes!"

"*That*," the dark-skinned girl said satisfactorily, "is a salvia trip."

Of all the shit that had just happened, I couldn't believe that it was the "millions of lives" part I chose to share. For some reason, that part stuck with me the most. As I sat on the deck, surrounded by spectators, the memories of my journey already began to flee from me. As real and intense as the trip had been, I didn't take it seriously. It was just a drug trip. It wasn't real.

"How long was I tripping?" I asked.

"Around five minutes," the bi hardware-store chick said. "You started crawling away at one point, like you were scared or something. We had to hold you down and try to explain that you were okay."

"Did I say anything?"

"No, you just looked concerned," she said and laughed.

The dark-skinned girl and the gay guy that had watched me from the beginning helped me up. I tested my legs and when I was confident I could walk back inside by myself, I shrugged off their arms and they let go.

"I need to go sit down," I said.

I walked into the living room and sat down on the couch. Someone brought me a blanket and I wrapped it around my lower body.

"That was crazy," I said. I dug my phone out of my pocket and sent the same text to about ten different people: "I just did salvia."

It's embarrassing. I'm not sure I realized it at the time, but I was showing off, trying to impress people and show them how wild and crazy I was. It still hadn't dawned on me that what I had just experienced would change my life forever. It wasn't a laughing matter, but I had a grin plastered to my face—just like after I'd fucked the hooker, except there wasn't any guilt this time.

Not yet.

I WOKE UP on the couch the next morning with a headache.

Oh, the joy of hangovers.

I sat up and stretched out the kinks in my arms and legs, then got up and looked around. Only two people still occupied the house—Katie's friend Grant, who lived there, and some guy I could only assume he'd slept with.

I heard them talking in a bedroom, so I walked over and peeked my head through the door.

"Hey, man, thanks for the party," I told Grant. "I'm going to head out."

"Hey," he said, a big grin on his face. "I heard you did salvia last night. Pretty crazy."

"Yeah," I said. "It was . . . it was weird. Really weird. Anyway, you guys have a nice day."

"You too."

I walked outside. The sun was bright, shining down on my face. I felt happy. All in all, last night had been pretty fun.

I got in my car and drove home.

# Panic

> All things began in order, so shall they end,
> and so shall they begin again.
> —Sir Thomas Browne

I SMOKED A LOT OF WEED WITH MY BROTHER AND HIS girlfriend that summer. A *lot*.

We sat around their kitchen table one lazy Saturday evening passing around a bong. My brother praised the quality of the weed.

"I think this is some of the best shit I've ever bought," Tim said.

"It definitely seems strong," I said after exhaling a plume of smoke. "I'm getting *really* baked." I challenged myself to hold in the weed for as long as I could. Tim was impressed.

"You know," he said, "I think Jason might actually be able to outsmoke *me*."

"Maybe," I said after exhaling another hit. Then again, maybe I was simply overindulgent.

"Do you guys hear that?" I asked.

Tim and Lisa exchanged a confused glance.

"Hear what?" Tim asked.

"Shh, be quiet for a second. Hear that?" I paused to let them listen. "Sirens."

They exchanged another look. "We don't hear anything," Tim said.

"Shit, I might be smoking *way* too much of this," I said. We all laughed.

The refrigerator caught my eye and I suddenly realized my stomach felt empty.

"I'm starving," I said. "Mind if I help myself to some of your food?"

"Sure, help yourself."

"Are you guys hungry?"

"Nah, we ate before you came over. But help yourself. We have some Hot Pockets in the freezer."

I grinned. "I *love* Hot Pockets!" I got up, opened the freezer, and grabbed a pizza-flavored Hot Pocket. I zapped it in the microwave, put it on a plate, and brought it back to the kitchen table, prepared to stab into it with a fork.

Just as I cut off the first piece with my fork and brought it to my lips, something happened.

A tingling sensation shot through my right thigh. I bolted upright.

It felt just like salvia.

The room spun. It didn't seem like reality was being stripped away layer by layer, but the déjà vu was unmistakable nonetheless.

## Panic

In fact, the sense of déjà vu was unceasing; it was as if the first déjà vu had set off another one, which set off another one, which set of another one . . . looking back on the experience, it reminded me of when I was a little boy visiting my great grandmother. Her bathroom had two mirrors facing each other: one right above the sink, and another placed on the opposite wall. I remember standing in front of one mirror and watching them reflect each other infinitely. A mirror within a mirror within a mirror within a mirror . . . In much the same way, I was stuck in an endless loop that was coming to a close and was about to start all over again. Time was beginning anew.

"Jason? Are you okay?" Tim asked.

I could barely move. I stood rigidly and turned to stare at Tim and Lisa in horror.

"Jason, what's wrong?" I didn't answer. I *couldn't* answer. Tim and Lisa laughed. "Oh man," Tim said, "he is so fucking baked. Jason. Jason! Man, he is freaking out."

I heard Tim's words, but I couldn't discern what he was saying. It all seemed like part of some ancient script. I felt like I'd already lived this exact moment billions of times. The universe had begun collapsing on itself. All matter in the universe had been condensed into this house and the three people in it. Soon Tim and Lisa would merge together, into one person, and then I would merge with them. The universe would collapse into an impossibly small point, erupt in a "big bang," and it would all start over again. It would take me eons to get back to this point, but it would all happen exactly the same way. My life would unfold exactly as it already had. My obsession with fitting in would lead me to abuse drugs and my drug abuse would land me in this kitchen with my brother and his girlfriend, awaiting the death and rebirth of the universe. It was the worst kind of predestination. I was helplessly stuck. Suicide wasn't an option. If it was, I would have killed myself already. I wanted this cycle to end, but it couldn't end. I knew it was a natural process. There wasn't somebody *making* this happen, it just *happened*. It had always happened like this and it always would. It was the way the universe worked.

"Wait, I think . . . there's something really wrong with him," Tim said, his amusement becoming concern. "Jason. Jason!" He grabbed my shoulders. "Jason!" I stared at him helplessly. I studied his face; I could see every detail of it, down to the individual pores. He shook me, but still, I stared helplessly. He slapped me once, then raised his hand again and backhanded the other cheek. I barely felt it. My face was numb. I stared ahead, horrified.

Thoughts raced through my head—impossible thoughts that didn't make any sense, that had nothing to do with my salvia trip, even though the experience seemed somehow exactly like my salvia trip.

My dad had done LSD once, back in the seventies, and he described it as "taking a trip without ever leaving the couch." The thought crossed my mind that maybe I *was* my dad; maybe my entire life was his LSD trip and he—I—was coming down now, about to find myself back on the couch.

A few weeks after doing salvia, I'd called Tim (who already knew I'd smoked salvia, as he was among the people I'd texted after doing so) and told him I thought I might still be tripping, that the sensation that the effects of the drug had worn off was merely part of the trip. Even though it had been days since I'd taken the drug, I thought maybe I was still sitting on that deck, mumbling incoherently and crawling away from my sitters, totally divorced from reality.

I'd been half-joking. But the thought had seriously crossed my mind. When I say that salvia divinorum made it impossible for me to trust reality, to trust my senses, I mean it. I'm not completely certain what's real anymore. As I sat there, feeling like I was tripping out again, I thought that maybe the trip was finally ending and I was awakening to a reality more terrifying than I could fathom.

For some strange reason, I also thought about race relations in the United States, internally lamenting the evils that had been committed throughout history based on the color of people's skin. I don't know why that thought entered my mind. It was like my brain was firing off random neurons. I wondered if I was dying.

I snapped out of it abruptly.

"HOLY SHIT!"

"Jason? What happened?"

"Holy shit!" I repeated. "That was just like salvia!"

I turned to look at Tim. His face was unreadable for the most part, but his brow was scrunched in concern. I turned to look at Lisa. She looked horror-stricken. She shook her head back and forth gently as if what I'd just said was absolutely insane.

"I'm—I'm sorry," I said apologetically. "I don't know what happened, I just . . . that was so intense . . ."

"You'd better sit down," Tim said. He started walking me to the living room, but I stopped him.

"I have to pee," I said. I was suddenly aware that my bladder was aching from the built-up pressure. That had happened before; I tended to be less aware of my bodily functions when stoned.

I could see Tim deliberate in his head for a moment. When he was through, he nodded his head in affirmation. "Alright," he said. "Go use the bathroom."

I locked myself in the bathroom, dropped my pants, and

squeezed my bladder, but nothing came out. I'd always had what's commonly referred to as a "shy bladder," which is basically when one is so anxious they can't urinate. Usually it's because someone's standing in the urinal next to them. It only made sense that after having what I could only describe as the first real panic attack of my life—which, I realized, I was still having—I would have a little trouble peeing.

I braced my left arm against the wall and strained. I swore at myself. My bladder felt like it was going to explode. Why couldn't I just *pee*?

There was a knock at the door.

"You okay?" Tim asked.

"Yeah," I said. "I'm just, uh . . . having a little trouble getting the flow going."

"Let me know if you need any, uh . . . help with anything."

It took me five minutes just to empty my bladder.

I emerged from the bathroom feeling a little calmer, although it still felt like my blood cells were using my veins as their own NASCAR track. I walked past Tim and Lisa in the kitchen, straight into the living room, and sat down on the couch.

"That was so weird," I said. "Are you sure that weed wasn't laced with something?"

"We smoked almost as much as you did, and nothing happened to us," Tim said.

"True. That was so *weird*, though." Apparently "weird" is the only word I could think of to describe anything associated with a drug trip. "I've never felt like that just from smoking weed before."

"How are you doing now?" Lisa asked.

"Better, but still freaked out. I thought the universe was ending." As I sat there, taking in the familiar surroundings, I began to feel déjà vu again, and although it was not nearly as intense as it had been earlier, it still sent a wave of panic through my body.

I jumped up and paced back and forth, rubbing my hands together frantically.

"Uh, Tim," I said, "I really need to get out of this house."

"You want to go outside?"

"No," I said quickly. "It's too dark out there. I'm already freaked out. That would only make things worse. No, uh . . . would you mind taking me on a drive?"

"A drive? Where?"

"Anywhere. Please, Tim," I said, a hint of desperation in my voice.

I could tell he was tired and driving was the last thing he wanted to do, but he was worried about me. "Alright, let me get my coat . . ."

We drove in silence, the darkness leading my thoughts to places I didn't want to visit. I sat in the back seat; Lisa decided to come with us. I asked Tim if he would put on some music. But as he started the CD player, I panicked.

"Make sure it's not Sublime," I said urgently. Earlier that day we'd driven into town listening to Sublime. It was too fresh, too familiar—if he played Sublime, it would mean the déjà vu would return, the universe would indeed end, and I would be unable to halt my demise.

Tim and Lisa exchanged another nervous glance at each other. They must have thought I couldn't see them, but I could, and it made me self-conscious.

"I'm not crazy," I said.

"I know you're not," Tim said. "We don't need to play Sublime." He gestured for Lisa to look through the glove box and she pulled out a cassette tape. "Here we go," Tim said. "Doo-wop."

It was perfect. I couldn't have picked out more comforting music myself. Doo-wop represented an earlier, more innocent time and, more importantly, a time before I was born. It helped remind me there was more to the universe than just me—and, thankfully, it didn't remind me *how much* more there was to the universe than me, making me feel insignificant, like my life didn't matter. It reminded me that simplicity, innocence and love all existed and that as soon as this night was over, I could go back to living a normal life. At least, I hoped I could.

"Are you hungry?" Tim asked.

"No, but I am thirsty." I suddenly realized my mouth felt rough and dry, like sandpaper. "I could use some water."

He pulled into the drive-through of a fast-food restaurant. I had calmed down considerably, and they both sensed it. The atmosphere in the car shifted from panicky—me from my salvia flashback, them from worrying about me—to fun, almost as if we were just cruising around town. Tim and Lisa decided to get milkshakes.

"You sure you don't want a shake or something to eat, Jason?"

"Just the water." I was dying of thirst. Water sounded like heaven.

He handed it to me and I sucked it down before we got out of the parking lot. I was still thirsty, but not nearly as much as I had been. Now that I'd hydrated a little, I felt even more like myself. By the time we got back to Tim's house, I had not only calmed down, I'd grown tired.

"Thanks a lot for driving me," I said. "I really appreciate it. I know it's late and everything."

"Don't worry about it."

Tim and Lisa walked into their bedroom and closed the door. I turned off the light, hopped onto the couch and instantly fell asleep.

# Research

> Real are the dreams of Gods, and smoothly pass /
> Their pleasures in a long immortal dream.
> —John Keats

WHEN I GOT BACK TO SCHOOL, I MOVED OUT OF THE DORM and into a small house with Joel, his girlfriend, and a friend of mine I'd met online named Lauren.

I tried not to think too much about salvia, but ever since the incident at Tim's house, the effort had become futile. It was *all* I could think about.

I was alone in my room one day surfing the internet. I typed "salvia" into a search engine and a ton of hits came up.

I found myself on a website called Salvia.net, and a tab called "Experiences" caught my eye. I clicked on it, and was taken to a page filled with dozens of typo-filled accounts of the batshit-crazy trips people had on salvia.

One salvia user identified as "Kurt" wrote that time, as well as his entire life, was revealed to be an illusion after he smoked the drug. He heard a female voice that reminded him of Morpheus from *The Matrix* ask if he wanted to stay chained to the illusory reality he was familiar with or jump further down the rabbit hole.

He shared the sensation I'd had that he'd been "duped" into thinking his life was real. Just like me, he felt his ego disappearing. He felt himself ceasing to exist. He, too, felt like he'd experienced it all before.

Someone identified as "Copehead" felt displaced from time. They felt like they existed in thousands of moments in the past and future, including moments from other people's lives. Although the trip felt real, they noted, as I had, that it was difficult to hang on to the memories of the experience.

Another person wrote that billions of people had gone through the experience before, and that each one was insignificant. Like me, like countless others, he felt tricked into nonexistence.

The similarities to my experience were eerie. No, not just eerie. Scary. My pulse quickened as I read the accounts. I could barely breathe. It felt like the start of a panic attack—just like the one I'd had in front of Tim and Lisa.

I leapt off my computer chair and flew out of my room into the kitchen for a glass of water.

Joel's girlfriend was washing dishes when I walked in. She must have noticed how pale I was. I must have looked like I'd seen a ghost. But I hadn't seen a ghost. I'd seen something much worse. I'd seen the insignificance of the universe.

"Are you okay?" she asked as I gulped down the water.

"Yeah," I answered when I finished. "I'm fine."

Then I walked back into my room and continued researching salvia.

# Research

I know Wikipedia should be the last place one goes for reliable information—my college professors drilled that fact into my head nearly every day—but I believe it's a great place to get a general overview of a topic, as long as you take everything with a grain of salt. So I looked up salvia on Wikipedia:

"*Salvia divinorum* (known colloquially by its genus name *Salvia*) is a psychoactive herb which can induce dissociative effects. It is a herbaceous perennial in the Lamiaceae (mint) family. The specific name, *Salvia divinorum*, was given because of its traditional use in divination and healing—it literally translates to 'diviner's sage' or 'seer's sage.'"

I wasn't sure what "dissociative" meant, and the word was hyperlinked, so I clicked on it and opened the link in a new browser tab:

"Dissociatives are a class of psychoactive drugs which are said to reduce or block signals to the conscious mind from other parts of the brain. Although many kinds of drugs are capable of such action, dissociatives are unique in that they do so in such a way that they produce hallucinogenic effects, which may include sensory deprivation, dissociation, hallucinations, and dream-like states or trances. Some which are nonselective in action and affect the dopamine and/or opioid systems may be capable of inducing euphoria. Many dissociatives have general depressant effects and can produce sedation, respiratory depression, analgesia, anesthesia, and ataxia, as well as cognitive and memory impairment and amnesia."

The part about "hallucinations and dream-like states or trances" definitely sounded like salvia. Now I was interested in other mind-altering drugs, and, after clicking on link after link, I eventually stumbled upon the Wikipedia entry for Dipropyltryptamine.

Dipropyltryptamine, or DPT, is a psychedelic drug sometimes used by the Temple of the True Inner Light, an offshoot of the Native American Church, in New York City. Wikipedia states that, "The Temple believes DPT and other entheogens are physical manifestations of God." However, the drug has never been found to occur naturally.

What really caught my interest was the section labeled "Psychedelic properties." The second to last paragraph in that section stated: "A user may also encounter the feeling of experiencing the life of someone else, or having had all possible experiences simultaneously."

I hadn't known how to put it into words, but that was *exactly* what I'd experienced on salvia! Not only had I felt like I'd lived millions of other people's lives, at one point, at the climax of the trip, I had felt as if I'd experienced every possible experience at the same time. The fact that this experience had been documented enough to find its way into a Wikipedia entry gave me goosebumps.

That was enough research for one night, I decided. I wanted to put salvia out of my mind for a while. I wanted to go out and get drunk.

That night, my phone rang. It was Roxy.

My heart pounded. It had been awhile since I'd talked to her. She had a boyfriend now and it didn't seem appropriate to hang out with her as much, especially considering the secret crush I'd harbored. The secret crush I was trying only somewhat successfully to get over.

"Hey Jason!" She sounded enthusiastic. I could hear chattering in the background. I put two and two together: she was drunk and she was at a party. "What are you doing?"

"Nothing much," I said.

# Research

"You should come here," she said. "Amber and I are at a party."

"Oh . . . um . . . yeah, that sounds fun," I said. I looked over at my roommate, Lauren, watching TV. "You mind if I bring my roommate along?"

"The more the merrier!" She gave me directions and I hung up.

"Hey Lauren," I said. "Wanna go to a party?"

AFTER A TEN-MINUTE drive that should have taken only five minutes (I got lost), we arrived at the party house.

I texted Roxy to let her know we were there and she answered the door.

"Hey, Jason!" she said, clearly drunk. She wrapped her arms around me. "I'm so glad you could make it!"

My heart raced at her touch, so I pulled back from the hug. "Roxy, this is my roommate, Lauren."

"Hey Lauren," she said.

"Hi," Lauren said shyly.

Amber emerged from behind Roxy and greeted us as we stepped inside. I closed the door behind us.

We walked upstairs. Roxy informed us there was a keg on the porch, so Lauren and I stepped outside to grab beers, then joined Roxy and Amber back in the kitchen. A bunch of other people were scattered about, speaking fervently. They already had alcohol in their systems.

As I drank, I loosened up a little and started talking to some people. But as Lauren drank, she started to dominate the conversation, and I found myself awkwardly holding back. I hated that feeling. Every once in a while, despite all the progress I'd made toward my goal of becoming a sociable person, I still sometimes found myself shutting down, unable to participate in conversations, just standing back and listening with a dumb smile on my face, looking like a fucking idiot.

But a strange thing happened. As the conversation turned philosophical, Lauren held up her shirt to reveal a tattoo on her back. It was a tattoo of a globe, accompanied by big, bold letters that read, "The world is an illusion."

My eyes widened. *Holy fucking shit*, I thought. *The world is an illusion . . . that's exactly what I experienced on salvia.*

"It's a Buddhist saying," she said. "I just thought it would make a cool tattoo."

It would more than make a cool tattoo, I thought. It could become a person's entire worldview. I hadn't just toyed around with the notion that the world, that my *life*, was an illusion. I had experienced it. I had stared at indisputable proof that I did not exist. I had been told that everything I'd believed was unequivocally an illusion.

After my salvia trip, I had initially assumed that my visions of reality being stripped away, and of a mysterious entity informing me that everything I'd believed was a lie, was merely a hallucination. Sure, it was disturbing, and sure, it was vivid and felt real. But it wasn't real.

But now I was having doubts. The experiences people described in their trip reports on Salvia.net bore numerous similarities to my experience. It was probably just a coincidence. But it didn't feel like a coincidence.

Then there was Lauren's tattoo—apparently a reference to Buddhism. What other religious and philosophical ideas might be unsettlingly similar to what I experienced on salvia?

I realized I had a lot more exploring to do.

# Early History

> Nothing is real.
> —THE BEATLES, "Strawberry Fields Forever"

SALVIA DIVINORUM, TRANSLATED LITERALLY, MEANS "SAGE OF the Seers." It is an entheogen—a class of substances defined by Wiktionary.com as a "psychoactive substance used for the purpose of inducing a mystical or spiritual experience," which puts salvia in the same company as psilocybin mushrooms, mescaline and DMT. It's also a perennial member of the mint family.

There is some debate as to whether salvia is a cultigen, meaning it exists only by the grace of humans who make an active effort to cultivate it, and not in the wild. Some people speculate that the plant is a hybrid, perhaps even one specifically cultivated into existence by human hands. What's not up for debate is the fact that salvia has played a spiritual role for the Mazatec Indians for centuries.

Like all good things, humanity has a way of perverting the meaningful for entertainment's sake. Salvia is no exception. In the last couple of decades, we have taken something somber and spiritual and turned it into a YouTube spectacle. How did it happen? How did a drug with a history spanning hundreds of years, that was used by shamans as a healing and divination tool and a gateway to a divine realm, become a way for snot-nosed teens to rack up YouTube views?

Let's start at the beginning. Or at least, as close to the beginning as we can get.

Nobody knows exactly how long the shamans, or *curanderos*, of the Mazatec people of Oaxaca, Mexico, have used *Salvia divinorum*, but it's been at least hundreds of years.

There's speculation that the plant was even used by the citizens of the Aztec Empire, which thrived in the 1400s and 1500s in present-day Mexico. One distinct aspect of Aztec culture was its reliance upon a variety of entheogens. Though many of these entheogens have been identified, one, called *pipiltzintzintli* (also known as *pepetichinque*) is a mystery. And while we may never know for sure what *pipiltzintzintli* is, some people say evidence points toward a prime suspect: *Salvia divinorum*. Additionally, some have interpreted[1] a depiction of the Mayan *Dresden Codex* as incorporating images of *Salvia divinorum* in the headdress of a deity. Skeptics, however, point to cannabis or morning glory as a more likely candidate for the identity of *pipiltzintzintli*.[2] Although we can't know for sure whether the Aztecs or the Mayans used salvia, it is clear that it has played an essential role in Mazatec culture.

The name "Mazatec" is a reference to Mazatlan—a Mexican city founded in 1531. Both names are derived from the Nahuatl

## Early History

word for deer, *mazatl*, with Mazatlan meaning "place of the deer," and Mazatec meaning "people of the deer." The Mazatecs are said to have been given their name by the Spanish when they came to Mexico and encountered the Mazatec people.

The Mazatecs practice a blend of Catholic Christianity—introduced by the Spanish—and their own traditional beliefs. This is evidenced by their name for salvia, *ska Maria Pastora*,* which means, "the herb of Mary, the Shepherdess." The Mazatecs believe salvia is an incarnation of the Virgin Mary, hence the name.[3] It's interesting to note that Mary is never depicted as a shepherdess in the Bible. This characterization appears to be unique to the Mazatecs.

For the Mazatecs, religion and healing are inexorably entwined, and the natives use a variety of substances considered illicit in the U.S. in the pursuit of spiritual and physical healing.[4] Foremost among them are psilocybin mushrooms,† although salvia and marijuana are also used.

Mazatec shamans learn their craft through an apprenticeship, although they consider themselves to be taught by "a progression of visions from and of heaven," according to IAmShaman.com. The apprenticeship can last more than two years, and psychotropic plants play a large role in the training.

---

* Also known as *Maria Pastora*, *Ska Pastora*, or *hojas de la Pastora* ("leaves of the shepherdess").

† Many reports indicate that the Mazatecs primarily use salvia as an alternative to psilocybin mushrooms when the mushrooms are out of season. This may sound odd to anyone who has experienced the intensity of a salvia trip, but it's important to keep in mind that these intense trips are typically brought about by extracts of salvia's active ingredient, salvinorin A. The Mazatecs ingest salvia by chewing the plant's leaves; the active ingredient is then absorbed through the mouth's mucous membranes. This method results in a trip that comes on more gradually and lasts longer than smoking salvia extract—but the effects are also decidedly less intense.

## Summer of Salvia

Typically, shamanic apprentices are at least thirty years old, as the job requires "maturity." During the training, an apprentice takes psychotropic substances anywhere from once a week to once a month, with the frequency tapering off after they've officially become a healer.

Shamanic apprentices begin by taking increasingly larger doses of *Salvia divinorum* to become familiar with the "way to heaven." The shamans must also master morning glory seeds—which contain the psychoactive substance d-lysergic acid amide, or LSA—as well as the hallucinogenic mushrooms. Apprentices must also adhere to a strict diet limiting spicy foods, alcohol and sexual activity.

*Salvia divinorum* didn't catch the attention of the western world until the 1930s. The first recorded mention of *Salvia divinorum* in modern, western history was reportedly made in 1938 by Jean B. Johnson, an American anthropologist who conducted field studies in Mexico throughout the 1930s and 1940s.[5] Johnson had heard that the Mazatec Indians made tea from the plant's leaves to induce visions.

Though Johnson merely made mention of salvia, we have two intrepid explorers to thank for making salvia more widely known in the western world (although it was their reports of psilocybin mushrooms that most vividly captured the public's attention). They are R. Gordon Wasson—an American banker with J.P. Morgan & Co.—and Swiss chemist Albert Hofmann, the discoverer of LSD.

Wasson and Hofmann brought back the first dried (not live) *Salvia divinorum* specimen after visiting the Mazatec region of Mexico in the autumn of 1962.

Wasson reportedly described drinking a mixture of juice from salvia leaves and water under the guidance of a Mazatec

# EARLY HISTORY

shaman as follows:[6]

"The effect of the leaves came sooner than would have been the case with the [psilocybin] mushrooms, was less sweeping, and lasted a shorter time. There was not the slightest doubt about the effect, but it did not go beyond the initial effect of the mushrooms—dancing colors in elaborate, three-dimensional designs."

In a 1976 interview with *High Times* magazine,[7] Hofmann said he and Wasson traveled to Mexico in search of salvia, then known only as a mysterious, "magic" Mexican plant called *hojas de la Pastora* (which means, "leaves of the shepherdess").

"We traveled by horseback on Indian trails through the Sierra Mazateca, finally arriving in time to assist in a nocturnal ceremony in the hut of a curandera, who used the juice of the leaves of *hojas de la Pastora*," Hofmann recalled in the interview. "Afterwards, we were able to get some specimens of the plant. It was a new species of the mint family that was later identified botanically at Harvard University and named *Salvia divinorum*."

Hofmann goes on to describe salvia's psychoactive effects as similar to those of psilocybin mushrooms, but "less pronounced."

There has been a general assumption that most *Salvia divinorum* plants in the United States today were propagated from cuttings of live plants brought back by Wasson and Hofmann, leading many people to refer to this strain of salvia as the "Wasson and Hofmann strain." On his website, Sagewisdom.org, salvia researcher and ethnobotanist* Daniel Siebert asserts that the strain was not, in fact, collected by Wasson and Hofmann, as previously believed, as all the samples Wasson collected were dried and pressed in Mexico. The proper credit, Siebert claims, belongs

---

* Ethnobotany is defined by Wikipedia as "the study of a region's plants and their practical uses through the traditional knowledge of a local culture and people."

to psychiatrist and ecologist Sterling Bunnell, who traveled to the Sierra Mazateca in June 1962 with poet, playwright and essayist Michael McClure.[8]

The main motivation for Bunnell and McClure for traveling to the Mazatec region of Mexico was to procure live cultures of psilocybin mushrooms for research at the Institute of Personality Assessment and Research (IPAR) at the University of California, Berkeley, Siebert writes. After returning to the Mazatecs several months after the initial expedition, in the fall of 1962, Bunnell obtained live specimens of salvia from a Mazatec shaman, and brought them back with him to California. He planted the specimens at his home—the first time *Salvia divinorum* was grown outside Mexico, according to Siebert. Bunnell also gave a pressed specimen to the UCLA herbarium—later relocated to Berkeley's herbarium. At the time, American botanist Carl Epling had not yet published his botanical description of the species, so its identity was not yet known, except to Epling, Wasson and a few close associates, Siebert writes.

Epling published a description of *Salvia divinorum* along with an ethnographic paper by Wasson a few days after Bunnel returned from Mexico, Siebert writes. Bunnell, upon seeing Epling's paper, met Epling in Los Angeles to give him the live specimens he had collected. Records show a live specimen of *Salvia divinorum* was entered into the collection of the UCLA Botanical Garden—now known as the Mildred E. Mathias Botanical Garden—in 1963. Bunnell also gave a specimen to Alexander Shulgin, then an employee for Dow Chemical in Walnut Creek, California.

The specimens Bunnell brought back were propagated and shared with other botanical gardens and botanists who continued to propagate them, according to Seibert, who asserts the strain should properly be called the "Bunnell strain." It was the first strain to become available commercially and remains the most widespread strain of *Salvia divinorum*, Siebert writes.

## MARIA SABINA

MARÍA SABINA WAS a Mazatec shaman who lived in Huautla de Jiménez, an Oaxacan mountain village. A lifelong Catholic, Sabina nevertheless retained her people's ancient traditions, serving as a *curandera*, or medicine woman, and partaking in both *Salvia divinorum*, and psilocybin mushrooms—which the Mazatecs call *'nti-ši-tho*, or "Little-One-Who-Springs-Forth," and which Sabina called "saint children."

It was Sabina who first allowed westerners to participate in the Mazatec *velada*, the all-night vigil in which participants ingest the mushrooms to heal sicknesses. It was she, in 1955, who introduced J. Gordon Wasson to psilocybin mushrooms and salvia.

Although the Mazatecs considered psilocybin mushrooms and *Salvia divinorum* sacred plants, their primary purpose was not as a religious tool, but rather as a healing medicine, according to a Timeline.com article.[9] The *velada* was meant to "commune with God to heal the sick."

"The spirits, if effectively contacted, would tell Sabina the nature of the sickness and the way it could be healed," the article states. "Vomiting by the afflicted was considered an essential part of the ceremony. Each participant in the ritual would ingest psilocybin mushrooms as Sabina (who typically ingested twice as much) chanted invocations to coax forth the divine."

In addition to healing the sick, the mushrooms could also be used to find things that had been lost. Sabina was reportedly reluctant to introduce Wasson, and a photographer who he had brought along, to the mushrooms, because he was not suffering from an illness. According to at least one account,[10] Wasson lied to Sabina, telling her he did not know the whereabouts of his son, and that he was concerned about his wellbeing. He later admitted he had deceived Sabina so he could participate in the ceremony.

Wasson eventually published an article in *Life* magazine about his visits to Oaxaca and his encounters with Sabina and the divine mushrooms.[11] The media attention resulted in an influx of western visitors to the Oaxaca region, many of whom also visited Sabina. This included celebrities such as Bob Dylan and John Lennon, as well as hordes of "beatniks" and "hippies." Though Sabina tended to be welcoming to the visitors, she emphasized the mushrooms' true purpose as a healing aid, as opposed to a means of achieving spiritual enlightenment.

Steve Beyer—who describes himself as an independent scholar researching ethnobotany, shamanism and hallucinogenic plants and fungi, among other things—quotes Sabina as saying, "Before Wasson nobody took the mushrooms only to find God. They were always taken for the sick to get well." Sabina, a Catholic, found God at Mass.

The other villagers blamed Sabina for the sudden deluge of westerners and their disregard for their proper use of the sacred mushrooms. Sabina was ostracized, her sterling reputation amongst those in her community forever tarnished. Her house was burned down and she drew unwanted attention from federal agents who accused her of selling drugs. Sabina, naturally, grew bitter toward the western visitors.

"But from the moment the foreigners arrived to search for God, the saint children lost their purity," Beyer quotes her as saying.[12] "They lost their force; the foreigners spoiled them. From now on they won't be any good. There's no remedy for it."

Wasson regretted his own role in perverting the use of the mushrooms, writing, "A practice carried on in secret for three centuries or more has now been aerated. And aeration spells the end."

Sabina died in 1985 at the age of ninety-one, completely penniless. Yet, she remains a popular figure and a draw to the region, her face plastered on T-shirts and other consumer products marketed to tourists.

## Modern History

> Salvia allows us to give up our senses and wander in the interdimensional time and space. Also, and this is probably hard for most to accept, our existence in general is pointless. Final point: Us earthly humans are nothing.
> —Brett Chidester

Sometime around the early- to mid-2000s, salvia started gaining popularity as a legal hallucinogen. The Associated Press story that sparked my interest in the drug pointed out that it was "more powerful than . . . peyote, psilocybin mushrooms or any other natural hallucinogen." And that was one of the less sensational stories on the subject. The *Ithica Journal* described salvia as "cheaper than marijuana, stronger than LSD,* as fast-acting as crack cocaine, and legally available to minors."

A study conducted from 2006-2009 reportedly showed a moderate increase in salvia use in the United States.[1] The study indicated that the lifetime prevalence of salvia use increased from .7 percent in 2006 to 1.3 percent in 2008. Those don't sound like large numbers, but it represents an 83 percent increase.

The study found that salvia use was most associated with white or multiracial men between the ages of eighteen and twenty-five. They tended to live in large, metropolitan areas. Many were depressed, and many had prior arrests for criminal activities. Common drug users were most likely to have used salvia. This included 54 percent of LSD users; 30 percent of ecstasy users; 24 percent of heroin users; 22 percent of phencyclidine† users; and 18 percent of cocaine users.

In fact, the past use of multiple drugs was the strongest indicator that someone had used salvia recently or in the past, the study found. About 43 percent of past salvia users, and

---

* LSD is actually considered more potent than salvinorin A. Most hallucinogenic drugs' psychotropic thresholds are measured in milligrams—10 milligrams for psilocybin, and 250 milligrams for mescaline, for example. LSD and salvinorin A are both measured in micrograms (for reference, 1 milligram is equal to 1,000 micrograms). LSD can produce noticeable effects with a dose of 50 micrograms. Salvinorin A is typically said to produce noticeable effects at between 100 and 500 micrograms. One study from the U.S. Department of Energy, however, found that salvinorin A produced noticeable effects in humans at just 10 micrograms, which would make it more potent than LSD. (More information on the study can be found at the beginning of the next chapter). It seems like there's a bit of a discrepancy, then, as to the minimum dosage of salvinorin A that produces psychoactive effects in humans. I'm not sure what the correct answer is—100 micrograms or 10 micrograms. But, either way, it's worth pointing out that LSD is a synthetic hallucinogen, while salvia is naturally occurring—which is why salvia is usually cited as the world's most powerful *naturally-occurring* hallucinogen, not the most powerful hallucinogen overall.

† PCP, or "Angel Dust"

## Modern History

29 percent of former salvia users had an "illicit or nonmedical drug-use disorder" compared with 2.5 percent of nonusers. Salvia users were also more likely to have been depressed in the past year, and to have a substance-use disorder involving alcohol or drugs, as opposed to users of alcohol or drugs who did not use salvia.

"The high prevalence of substance use disorders among recent *S. divinorum* users emphasizes the need to study health risks of drug interactions," the study authors write in their conclusion.

A 2011 study found use of *Salvia divinorum* to be prevalent among "recent or active drug users," particularly those who had used hallucinogens or stimulants. The study states that there is a high prevalence of substance abuse disorders among recent salvia users, highlighting the need to "study health risks of drug interactions."[2]

Despite sensationalist news stories depicting salvia as a potential public health hazard, the drug has come nowhere near epidemic status, and for good reason: Very few people continue using salvia after they've tried it. Salvia trips are intense and can be intensely unpleasant, especially for people who go into the experience unprepared or thinking salvia is some kind of party drug, which it decidedly is not.

Salvia isn't something one tries and becomes addicted to; it's a novelty you try once and tell your friends about. The prevalence of online stores supplying the drug helped get it in people's hands; head and smoke shops also started carrying the drug. People can choose from dried leaves or extracts. It's even possible to buy live salvia plants online for the botanically adventurous. Those with an extraordinarily gifted green thumb can even purchase salvia seeds—which are very rare, as the plant almost never grows from seed.

A 2005 study[3] published in the journal *Pharmacopsychiatry* concluded that salvia could become "increasingly attractive" to adolescents and young adults for the following reasons:

- It can be ordered at an affordable price.
- Its use promises "philosophical insights or escapism for young people seeking their own personality." Salvia use could also be seen as entry into a "community" of other salvia users, making the drug "socially attractive."
- Websites offer "a mixture of esoteric advice, practical warnings and instructions on the use of the plant." Consumers may take such information as "'evidence-based' in a scientific sense," and "underestimate known and unknown health risks."

Some articles promulgate the idea that salvia became popular as a legal alternative to marijuana, but this appears to be a lazy explanation. Marijuana prohibition in the United States is nothing new. It's been going strong since the early 1900s, yet salvia use has only become popular in the last two decades.

Secondly, the effects of salvia couldn't be further from those of marijuana. It's possible that some naïve teenagers have pursued salvia as a legal alternative to marijuana, but the idea that that accounts for the notable rise in the number of people using salvia doesn't quite add up. Some speculate that salvia's popularity will wane as efforts to legalize marijuana gain traction. But I think a more likely scenario is that salvia use will wane simply because salvia's use as a recreational drug is a fad and, like all fads, it will fade into relative obscurity, used only by those seeking divine, profound truths from the mind-bending trips they experience.

# Modern History

## YouTube and Miley Cyrus

A MAJOR CONTRIBUTOR to the rise in salvia use was YouTube. One study found that literally hundreds of videos of teenagers of young adults tripping out on salvia have been posted to YouTube.[4] This is only my speculation, but it makes sense that these infamous YouTube videos would make more people aware of salvia, both because more people stumbled upon the videos, and because more people were reading the numerous, alarmist news stories which popped up in response. Surely, many of these people were enticed to try the drug after hearing about it. And if they, in turn, told their friends about it or posted their own videos, it led to even more people becoming aware of and trying the drug.

Many people heard about salvia for the first time because of its association with pop star Miley Cyrus, better known back then as Hannah Montana.

In December 2010, a video surfaced of Cyrus, freshly eighteen, taking a hit off a bong. The video's release was an instant scandal. At the time, Cyrus was considered a model pop star; innocent, virtuous and a perfect role model for young girls. Her show, *Hannah Montana*, aired on the Disney Channel, as family-friendly a network as they come.

The idea that this virtuous celebrity would dare be caught in the same room as a bong rocked the sensibilities of moralistic parents across the country, and they worried about how the fall of such a beloved role model would affect their children. The incident also attracted the attention of scandal-loving—and generating—media outlets like *TMZ* (which first obtained and released the video). *TMZ* noted in its initial report that it was salvia—not marijuana, as many initially assumed—in the bong, noting that it is a "natural herb . . . which has psychedelic qualities," and adding that it is legal in California.[5] (It's still legal in California, but selling it to minors is prohibited).

After the video was released, Cyrus reportedly told *Marie Claire* magazine, "I made a mistake . . . I'm disappointed in myself for disappointing my fans."[6] That statement reeks of publicist-ordered damage control, especially considering the trajectory Cyrus' career has taken since then—she quickly shed her "good girl" image in favor of a more provocative sensibility. But this encounter with salvia was the first step in Cyrus' descent into "bad girl" territory.

Cyrus' personal drama aside, news of the incident went viral, briefly catapulting salvia into the public spotlight. The once-obscure shamanic plant is even referenced every now and then in popular culture.

For instance, in the fourth-season episode of the cartoon *American Dad*, "Roy Rogers McFreely," the character Hayley rips open her shirt to reveal what she thinks is going to be some kind of protest symbol painted on her bare chest, only to find the "Ghostbusters 2" logo painted there instead. "I gotta stop smoking salvia before I go to the body-painting place," she says. The joke doesn't really make sense, but it demonstrates the exposure the drug had in pop culture at the time.

Further evidence of the Cyrus controversy's role in spreading awareness of *Salvia divinorum* can be seen in the spike in sales of the drug after *TMZ* broke the story. The day after publishing the Miley Cyrus video, *TMZ* reported that sales of salvia were through the roof, possibly even tripling overnight.[7] To be fair, the report is based on anecdotal evidence from retail outlets selling the drug, but it seems apparent there was some boost in sales, even if the full extent of that boost may have been exaggerated.

# Modern History

While YouTube and Miley Cyrus may have helped propel salvia into the public consciousness, the name that deserves the most credit for putting the drug on people's radar—especially that of legislators—was an unassuming teen from Delaware whose salvia use, according to his mother, prompted him to take his own life.

## Brett Chidester

IN JANUARY 2006, seventeen-year-old Brett Chidester of Newark, Delaware, hauled his father's charcoal grill into a tent and zipped himself inside it. He lit the grill and waited to die of asphyxiation.

Kathleen and Dennis Chidester placed the blame for their son's suicide squarely on *Salvia divinorum*.

"He told his girlfriend that he felt [salvia] was addictive and that he wasn't able to stop," Kathleen Chidester said, according to an article in *PC World* magazine.[8] "He also told her the night before he died that he felt there was something wrong with him, but he couldn't figure out what it was. I believe the use of salvia was reshaping Brett's mind, distorting how he viewed himself and the world around him. I think he just snapped."

Though an autopsy showed no traces of salvia or any other illicit drugs in Brett's system, police officers investigating his death found salvia in his truck, and *Salvia divinorum* was listed as a "contributing cause of his death" on his death certificate. It's not clear from reports what form of salvia Brett used—whether it was dried leaves, salvinorin A extract, or something else.

According to the *PC World* article, Chidester left behind eight notes. In one, he reportedly wrote, "Salvia makes me realize that humans have no reason to be on Earth. We are all just grains of sand on reality beach." It was a haunting conclusion that countless other salvia users have reached (which is explored more in the chapter titled, "Philosophy.")

In the wake of her son's death, Kathleen Chidester began pushing for a ban on *Salvia divinorum*. "I don't believe Brett's was the first salvia-related suicide, and I don't believe his will be the last," she said.

Kathleen first found success banning salvia with "Brett's Law." Three months after her son's death, the Delaware legislature signed the namesake legislation into law. It was sponsored by Delaware Senator Karen Peterson, and it classified *Salvia divinorum* as a Delaware Schedule I controlled substance. Possession, use or consumption of the drug is a class B misdemeanor under the law.

At the time of this writing, *Salvia divinorum* is not a federally controlled substance in the United States (although the DEA does list it as a "drug of concern"[9]), but around 30 states have passed legislation prohibiting the possession and/or use of salvia.

Worldwide, salvia is illegal to possess or sell in nineteen countries:[10] Australia, Belgium, Canada, Croatia, the Czech Republic, Denmark, Germany, Hong Kong, Ireland, Italy, Japan, Latvia, Lithuania, Poland, Portugal, Romania, South Korea, Sweden and Switzerland.

Additionally, it is illegal to sell, but legal to possess, in Chile, France and Spain. It is illegal to grow or sell, but legal to possess, in Russia, and is treated as a medicinal herb requiring a prescription in Estonia, Finland, Iceland and Norway.

There is no evidence that salvia is habit-forming, and overdose deaths from salvia are impossible. Though critics of Kathleen Chidester's war on salvia are quick to point out that there are no other deaths linked to salvia, that's not entirely true.

## Modern History

My personal research shows no known salvia-related suicides except for Chidester's, although there is one unusual incident that might be an exception.

In March 2008, forty-two-year-old Mario G. Argenziano, a restaurant manager from Yonkers, New York, reportedly shot himself in the face ten minutes after smoking salvia.

Argenziano's wife, Anna Argenziano, said her husband picked up a handgun from a bedside table to show some friends, then pointed it at himself and seemed confused, according to the *New York Times*.[11]

"Before the shot was fired, he was laughing," she reportedly said. She said her husband had no psychiatric history and Yonkers police said they couldn't determine what role salvia may have had in Argenziano's death, if any. Argenziano's death was certainly self-inflicted, but does it rise to the level of suicide? I'm not sure. But one could perhaps classify his death as a salvia-related suicide or accidental death.

More common, though still rare, are salvia-related accidents in which people under the influence of salvia fall to their deaths from open windows or other heights.

On March 6, 2011, twenty-one-year-old Ryan Santanna fell from a fifteenth-floor balcony of an apartment building in Roosevelt Island, New York. Roosevelt Islander Public Safety Department Director Keith Guerra said in a statement that, "Further investigation revealed that he was allegedly smoking Salvia and ran out onto the balcony and jumped. . . . The investigation revealed that it was a suicide, and the body was removed by the NYC (New York City) Coroner."[12]

Ryan's sister, Carolyn, claimed that her brother would have never committed suicide, and blamed her brother's death entirely on salvia, according to local news reports.[13] Carolyn said Ryan's girlfriend was with him when he smoked salvia and ran off the balcony. She gave a local news station the following account of what happened when the girlfriend ran into the room:

"She ran into my room screaming he jumped and I thought it was a joke. She stared [sic] crying so I ran to the balcony and looked down and I ran to my dad's room and woke him up and all he could scream was 'Ryan! Ryan! Ryan!'"

The girlfriend reportedly gave the following account: "Ryan Santanna dissolved into a fit of laughter about 2 minutes after smoking salvia, says the girlfriend who watched him do it. He made animal noises, looked at her as if he couldn't see her, pushed her inside the apartment, and then ran and jumped over the balcony."

Almost three months later, another salvia-related accident occurred in London.

On May 30, 2011, seventeen-year-old Rikki Green smoked salvia, and then jumped out of a window in London.[14] He sustained severe brain damage and died a week later, on June 6.

Green had reportedly taken the drug at an apartment belonging to one Nicholas Ford after he was given the drug.

"Within 10 seconds after he . . . took salvia he slumped backwards in his chair," Ford reportedly said. "He then started walking around the flat before lying down on the floor in the hallway. I asked if he was okay and Keith said to leave him alone, so as not to panic him. We assumed he was going to the toilet. I heard the door to my bedroom move so I went through and saw his feet disappear out of the window."

Green's aunt, Dawn Knight, reportedly criticized Ford and a friend for leaving the teenager in the hallway, insisting that he should have been supervised.

These deaths illustrate the importance of having a sitter—

someone to take care of you while tripping—when doing salvia, or any hallucinogenic drug for that matter. In Santanna's case, even though he was with his girlfriend, there were hazards that could have been avoided—if, for instance, he had consumed the drug on the ground level, or if they had made sure ahead of time to secure all windows and doors leading outside. In Green's case, proper supervision could have prevented the tragedy that ended his life.

## JARED LOUGHNER

AROUND TEN O'CLOCK in the morning on January 8, 2011, twenty-two-year old Jared Lee Loughner opened fire on a group of people outside a Safeway grocery store in Tucson, Arizona. Loughner's intended target, third-term democratic U.S. representative Gabrielle Giffords, was making a public appearance at the store.[15]

Giffords was shot in the head, but survived, and made an astounding recovery following several surgeries and intensive rehabilitation. But Loughner shot nineteen other people, killing six of them, including a federal judge.[16]

This was a big news story, and the media, as it always does, gathered every detail about Loughner it could get its hands on, even if it only had peripheral relevance to the shooting. One of the most startling pieces of information the media reported about Loughner was that he had been known to use *Salvia divinorum*.

As the *New York Times* points out, nobody seriously suggested that Loughner's use of salvia was directly responsible for his decision to murder six people in cold blood.[17]

"Yet it is striking," the paper wrote, "how closely the typical effects of the herb, Salvia divinorum—which federal drug officials warn can closely mimic psychosis—matched Mr. Loughner's own comments about how he saw the world, like his often-repeated assertion that he spent most of his waking hours in a dream world that he had learned to control."

Though the claim that the effects of salvia "closely mimic psychosis" is rather dubious, it's interesting to note the similarities between Loughner's assertion that he lived in "a dream world" and countless other salvia reports that suggest that the waking world is illusory. I haven't been able to find any detailed reports of Loughner's salvia trips.

The *New York Times* account goes on to state that Loughner was, at one time, a "frequent user" of salvia. He began smoking it in high school while also experimenting with marijuana, psilocybin mushrooms and other drugs. The paper claims mental health professionals say the drug can "both aggravate and mask the onset of mental illness." It isn't clear when Loughner last smoked salvia before he carried out his attack.

It's obvious that Loughner was not under the influence of salvia on that fateful January morning. If he had been, he wouldn't have been able to hold a gun, much less fire one.

What's less clear is whether salvia played a role in exacerbating the obvious mental illness that prompted him to carry out such a horrific act. The fact is, although scientists are learning more about how salvia affects the brain, there is still much we don't know about the drug's long-term effects.

## WORTH A BAN?

YOU'D BE HARD pressed to find a salvia user who advocates banning the plant—even those who report having bad trips.

A *Reason* magazine article describing efforts to ban *Salvia divinorum* solicited comments on Salvia's connection to Brett Chidester's suicide.[18]

Daniel Siebert says in the article that although salvia "might have influenced [Brett Chidester's] thinking in some way," he must have already had thoughts about committing suicide.

"Mentally healthy people don't decide to take such a drastic action based on [an idea] they had during a drug state," Siebert says. "Psychedelics basically amplify a lot of your own internal stuff. If you're already having some kind of dark thoughts, a psychedelic experience could amplify that, and it could lead to a problem for some people."

Richard Glen Boire, a senior fellow at the Center for Cognitive Liberty & Ethics, told the magazine that the theory that Chidester killed himself due to the disturbing revelations he had while on the drug "could apply to some of the greatest pieces of art in the history of the world. It would make Nietzsche a controlled substance. There is a lot of cultural production out there that shows a way of looking at the world that isn't all sunny and rosy."

On the subject of whether salvia could prompt someone to commit suicide, I can only speak for myself. Salvia transformed my life. In many ways, that transformation was not for the better. It led me to some of the same frightening conclusions Brett Chidester came to, and the existential dread that accompanies such thoughts has adversely affected my mental health. Among other efforts, one of the ways I've dealt with those issues is by writing this book. I have never seriously contemplated committing suicide. But each individual is different, and what one person can cope with by writing a book no one will read, another person may not be able to stand. But does that warrant an all-out ban on *Salvia divinorum*? I'm not convinced government regulation is the solution to the problem.

For one thing, a ban could block research on salvia. Despite its intense hallucinogenic effects, salvia shows promise as a treatment for a variety of maladies, including depression and opiate addiction.

Furthermore, history has shown that, even if we were to say drugs such as salvia are objectively bad (a proposition which is far from true, but we'll accept it for arguments' sake), prohibition would be a terrible way to protect people from it. It's plain that the so-called war on drugs has done more harm than good to our society. What is a better solution? I don't know for sure, but I think legalizing drugs, taxing them and funneling the tax money directly into addiction treatment centers would be a good start.

When I first took *Salvia divinorum*, all I really knew about it was that it produced hallucinations, and that those hallucinations only lasted for five to ten minutes. I had no idea how intense those hallucinations would be, or that the drug was also a dissociative. I didn't realize it would cause me to literally question the reality of my life every single day, eight years after I took it and counting.

If I'd known the psychological risks before taking the drug, perhaps I wouldn't have taken it. Education, not regulation, is the key to preventing another salvia-related suicide—as unlikely as such a suicide is. I hope this book will serve, at least for some people, as that education.

# Science

*A hallucination is a fact, not an error;
what is erroneous is a judgment based upon it.*
—BERTRAND RUSSELL

SALVIA DIVINORUM'S ACTIVE INGREDIENT IS CALLED
salvinorin A, and it targets the brain's kappa opioid receptors.[1] Although the kappa opioid receptors are known to modulate pain, they are different receptors than those targeted by other hallucinogens, or by opiates, such as morphine and codeine.

A 2008 study by the U.S. Department of Energy's Brookhaven National Laboratory found the effects of salvia were localized to the cerebellum and visual cortex, which control motor function and vision.[2] Just 10 micrograms of salvia in the brain causes psychoactive effects in humans, the study found.

The researchers used positron emission tomography scanning—or PET scanning—to see how low doses of radioactively-labeled salvinorin A traveled through the brains of anesthetized primates. The researchers found peak concentration of salvinorin A in the brain within forty seconds after administering the drug. That's nearly ten times faster than the rate cocaine enters the brain. Sixteen minutes after the drug was administered, it was "essentially gone."

"This pattern parallels the effects described by human users, who experience an almost immediate high that starts fading away within 5 to 10 minutes," the study states.

Alfredo Ortega first discovered salvinorin A in 1982 while researching novel terpenoid compounds in the salvia genus of plants.[3] His research did not explore salvia's psychoactive effects, however.

It was a group led by Leander Valdes that discovered that salvinorin A was the psychoactive component of the plant, when he isolated 39 grams of salvinorin A and injected it into mice. Valdes' experiments did not include testing on humans, however, and the group was not aware of the powerful effects the compound has on the human brain.

One of the leading experts on salvia, Dr. Bryan Roth, a professor of pharmacology at the University of North Carolina medical school, is reportedly the person who discovered that salvinorin A stimulates a single brain receptor[4]—the kappa upload receptor, which is believed to be linked to "interoception, pain sensing, mood and consciousness," according to a *Newsweek* article. This is in sharp contrast to other drugs, such as LSD, which stimulates around 50 receptors in the brain.

Additionally, salvia doesn't affect the brain's serotonin levels, unlike many drugs.

Salvinorin A is both a hallucinogen, which induces hallucinations in users, as well as a dissociative, meaning it makes the user feel as though they are dissociating not only from their surroundings, but often from themselves.[5] One way of putting this is that the user experiences "ego death"*—the death of their persona, their identity.

Daniel Siebert was the first person to realize the potency of salvinorin A after smoking an extract he had made in June 1993. Siebert had been smoking the dried leaves, but found that smoking the extract opened up a "vaster dimension," according to Erowid, a nonprofit organization that provides information about psychoactive substances.[6]

"He began a series of experiments producing concentrated extracts and trying various methods of administration," Erowid states. "During his experiments, Siebert felt the plant's spirit was issuing a kind of intuitional guidance, encouraging him to continue with the extraction process and discover a means of achieving a full Salvia experience."

Siebert describes his discovery in an article on his website titled, "Salvinorin A: The Breakthrough."[7]

Siebert had been working to isolate the compound in salvia responsible for its psychoactive effects. On June 6, 1993, he isolated 2.5 milligrams of an "unidentified impure crystalline fraction of *Salvia divinorum*," which was later shown to be made up of between 70 and 80 percent salvinorin A.

Siebert writes that he initially assumed the crystalline material he'd isolated from the plant was not psychoactive. He was about to throw it away when he decided at the last minute to test it just in case it proved to be psychoactive after all.

Placing the material on a piece of aluminum foil and vaporizing it with a torch lighter, he inhaled the fumes through a piece of glass tubing. After waiting a moment, he determined the

---

* Wikipedia defines ego death as a "complete loss of subjective self-identity."

material was, indeed, inactive.

But before he could scrap the rest of the substance, he suddenly found himself in a "confused, fast moving state of consciousness with absolutely no idea where my body or my universe had gone."

The initial confusion must have only lasted a few minutes, but to Siebert, it felt like an eternity. It felt like something had "gone wrong," and he wanted to return to the "real" world, he writes. He didn't remember being under the effect of any substances, and he struggled to remember what his house looked like, and even what his own body felt like. But the more he tried to cling to his reality, the more he realized there was nothing to cling to.

"At some point I realized that what I was trying to get back to did not exist—it was just an ephemeral dream," he writes. "At this point I realized that I had no actual memory of ever having existed in any other state of consciousness than the disembodied one I was now in. So I decided to stop panicking and just relax. After all, there was no place to get back to. I was totally convinced that this state of existence was all there ever was."

When he returned to the "real" world, and the effects of the substance wore off, Siebert realized he had made an important discovery.

Grabbing a pen, he wrote down his first impression of the experience:

"IT IS TOTAL MADNESS."

He followed that up with: "TEARING APART THE FABRIC OF REALITY. This is tooooooooo strong. It is tearing apart the fabric of existence. It is madness. Thank god it only lasted 10-15 minutes!"

He tried to calm himself, but to no avail. "I had been shaken to the soul," he writes.

# Science

## Salvia as Medicine

THE IDEA OF *Salvia divinorum* as a medicine is not new. The Mazatec Indians have been using it for healing purposes for hundreds of years. But they've used it in a shamanic sense, relying more on tradition and faith than on scientific research.

That's changing. Salvia's popularity amongst thrill-seeking teenagers and young adults has helped it catch the attention of scientific researchers as well.

Studies have explored salvia's potential for treating a host of ailments and disorders, including Alzheimer's disease, chronic pain and depression. Though it's unlikely salvinorin A would be used to treat maladies itself, because of its intense psychoactive effects, derivatives based on the drug's chemistry could be used as a potent, effective medicine.[8]

Salvia may also be a promising treatment for drug addiction. A 2014 study published in *Advances in pharmacology* looked at salvia's potential for treating cocaine abuse, and noted that salvinorin A is a "compound of high therapeutic promise in treating drug abuse."[9]

A research review published in 2014 notes that salvinorin A has demonstrated "anti-addiction effects in animal models using psychostimulants by attenuating dopamine release, sensitization, and other neurochemical and behavioral alterations associated with acute and prolonged administration of these drugs."[10]

A John Hopkins University study[11] published in the journal *Drug and Alcohol Dependence* showed that salvia had "no physically adverse effects on otherwise healthy people," though it noted that the intensity of the drug, and the possible behavioral hazards that accompany it, are another matter.

Matthew W. Johnson, the lead researcher for the study and a

psychologist and assistant professor of psychiatry, told *ABC News* that a "longer-acting version of the drug and one without the strong psychedelic effects, just the analgesic effects," could have great potential to treat disorders such as drug addiction.

Johnson told the news outlet that salvia's stimulus of the kappa opioid receptors—as opposed to the mu opioid receptors which opioids such as heroin and morphine target—has "the opposite of an addictive effect." With an opioid addiction epidemic sweeping through the United States, any non-addictive alternatives for pain management and other maladies should be embraced by researchers and lawmakers alike.

The United States Food and Drug Administration hasn't approved salvia for any medical use, but considering that the FDA also hasn't approved cannabis—a drug with myriad well-documented medical uses—for any medical use, the agency's stamp of approval, or lack thereof, is essentially meaningless.

## Ways to Take Salvia

THERE ARE A variety of ways to take *Salvia divinorum*—although that wasn't always the case.

The Mazatec Indians had two methods of taking salvia: chewing the leaves or drinking a juice made by steeping the leaves in water.

Of the two methods, the former is the most effective, because it gives the juices of the leaves the opportunity to be absorbed by the mouth's mucous membranes, which is how the active ingredient is ingested. When one simply drinks the leaf-juice mixture, the active ingredient is broken down in the gastrointestinal system and rendered mostly inert.

Nowadays, there are several other ways to take salvia, most

## Science

of which involve sucking smoke or vapor into your lungs. When taken the traditional way, by chewing the leaves, the effects of *Salvia divinorum* come on slowly, and last longer than by smoking or vaporizing it. When salvinorin A extract is smoked, the effects can come on quickly, in as little as thirty seconds, and the effects usually last anywhere from five to fifteen minutes. Taking the drug this way also results in a much more intense experience than you'd get chewing on the dried leaves.

Let me throw in a disclaimer here: I am not actively promoting *Salvia divinorum* or encouraging you (or anyone) to use it. If you choose to use *Salvia divinorum* in any way, you do so at your own risk. That being said, if you're interested in more information about the different methods of ingesting the drug, strictly for informational purposes, here you go:

**Bong.** Although you can smoke salvia in a standard-order pipe, it's generally recommended that you use a water pipe or bong when smoking the dried leaves. Daniel Siebert recommends using the combination of a torch lighter and water pipe.[12] The extra heat generated by torch lighters necessitates the water-cooling abilities of water pipes, he writes.

**Vaporizing.** Siebert recommends against vaporizing pure salvinorin A, writing that it's easy to vaporize too large a dose.[13]

**Drinking Juice.** Though the Mazatecs traditionally drank water infused with the juice of *Salvia divinorum* leaves, research by Daniel Siebert has found this to be the least effective method of ingesting *Salvia divinorum's* active ingredient, salvinorin A. This is because salvinorin is broken down in the gastrointestinal system. To the degree that this method does work, it is because salvinorin A is absorbed through the mouth's mucous membranes. Chewing on the leaves is a more effective alternative.

**Chewing Leaves.** Mazatec Indians roll up a ball of fresh or dried *Salvia divinorum* leaves, called a "quid." The user chews the quid slowly for about a half hour, keeping the liquid that forms in their mouth. This is important, because the active ingredient, salvinorin A, is absorbed through the mucous membranes in the mouth, not through the gastrointestinal system. After a half hour, the quid and the juice from the leaves can be spit out. The full effects are typically felt within a half hour and last anywhere from thirty minutes to an hour longer.[14]

**Tincture.** *Salvia divinorum* can be taken as a tincture—an alcohol-based liquid extract. Users should drop about 10 milliliters of the tincture under the tongue and hold the liquid there as long as possible. The effects begin in around ten to fifteen minutes, and the effects last for a total of around one hour.[15]

# Philosophy

> Have you ever had a dream, Neo, that you were so sure was real? What if you were unable to wake from that dream? How would you know the difference between the dream world and the real world?
> —Morpheus, *The Matrix*

After reflecting on Lauren's freaky Buddhist tattoo for a while, I had finally managed to put salvia out of my mind for a couple weeks. It returned soon enough when a book in the bargain bin at the bookstore caught my eye. It was called, *Is There Life After Death?* by Anthony Peake.

I figured it was probably filled with clichés about life and death and wishy-washy ideas about heaven and hell that couldn't provide me with any new insights or information. But the subtitle caught my interest: *The extraordinary science of what happens when we die*. I was intrigued to see what science said on the matter; was it possible that there was scientific evidence to support the notion of an afterlife? Did Peake have evidence to buoy my crippled faith? Would this book refute all the horrible notions about the nature of reality that salvia had put in my head?

I picked up the book and read the description on the back cover: "Life is not what it seems—Do you occasionally have that strange feeling known as déjà vu?" The smug smile I'd been wearing melted off my face. Life *wasn't* what it seemed—and I'd had more déjà vu since doing salvia than I'd had in my entire life. I read on: "Do you sometimes feel that you know what is going to happen next? Do you ever have a strong feeling that actions you are about to take are the right (or wrong) thing to do? All these perceptions may be everyday clues to your immortality. This book proposes a simply amazing theory, based upon solid scientific evidence: a theory that states your personal death is a scientific impossibility."

I bought the book.

When I came home, I went straight to my bedroom, hopped into bed, and cracked the book open.

"What made you pick up this book?" Peake writes in the prologue. "What series of events brought about the circumstances whereby you are reading these words? And why this book and not the dozens of others that you could have chosen? It is possible that you were guided by a power that you are, at present, only vaguely aware of—a power that has guided your life to this point, to have you looking down on this page and wondering what these words mean."

I was instantly intrigued. As I continued reading, Peake laid out a seemingly insane theory. It's a philosophy most people would dismiss as metaphysical nonsense—that *I* would have dismissed as metaphysical nonsense before I took salvia—and I found myself tumbling, as they say, down the rabbit hole.

Peake basically argues that the world *is* an illusion. That it's literally some kind of holographic construct—similar to the computer-generated world of *The Matrix* (in fact, Peake references *The Matrix* several times in his book).

Peake also argues that we relive our lives over and over again, kind of like reincarnation, except instead of being reborn and living a *different* life, we live the *same* life over and over and over again. And while it's more or less the exact same life, each time we relive it, he argues, we can make changes. This opportunity to change our lives is, in fact, the reason this endless cycle exists in the first place. So maybe when we live the perfect life, when we find the perfect combination of actions to get us what we want, ala *Groundhog Day* (another film Peake references), we'll finally be satisfied and the endless cycle will, paradoxically, come to an end. Of course, who knows what will happen then? Who knows what reality is like outside of the faux-reality we experience every day?

Peake also argues that, upon death, our consciousness is split in two. As we relive our lives, one part of our consciousness, called our *Daemon*, exists outside of the construct we call reality, in the outer, "true" reality, guiding our subconscious minds as we go through life again, thinking it's the first time we've done so. Peake calls the other part of our consciousness, the part that isn't aware of our reincarnation, the *Eidolon*. The Daemon knows what's coming, because it's lived this life before. It's the little voice in our heads telling us that something is a bad idea, because it knows the consequences of our actions—it's already experienced those consequences firsthand. The Eidolon moves through life ignorant of its eternal existence, except when it's able to tune into guidance from the Daemon.

As I read Peake's view of the universe, the parallels to my salvia trip frightened me. There had definitely been a sense that I'd lived my life before, and the déjà vu I kept experiencing afterward only seemed to reinforce that unsettling notion. And it wasn't just *my* salvia trip. Countless others had concluded that the world was an illusion after smoking salvia. That very notion had contributed to Brett Chidester's suicide. If you don't exist, then killing yourself doesn't really matter.

Peake's theory sounds disturbingly similar to another theory I stumbled across by philosopher and futurologist Nick Bostrom, a faculty member at the University of Oxford.

In 2003, Bostrom published a paper in *Philosophical Quarterly* magazine, titled, "Are You Living in a Computer Simulation?"[1]

Bostrom summarized his argument in the paper's abstract: "This paper argues that at least one of the following propositions is true: (1) the human species is very likely to go extinct before reaching a 'posthuman' stage; (2) any posthuman civilization is extremely unlikely to run a significant number of simulations of their evolutionary history (or variations thereof); (3) we are almost certainly living in a computer simulation. It follows that the belief that there is a significant chance that we will one day become posthumans who run ancestor-simulations is false, unless we are currently living in a simulation."

It's a question that took on an unusual importance in my life after doing salvia. Could it be that we are, indeed, living in a computer simulation, and that salvia somehow allowed me to see our universe, momentarily, for what it was: a digital sham?

In his paper, even Bostrom seems to recognize the religious and metaphysical implications inherent in this theory: "The argument provides a stimulus for formulating some methodological and metaphysical questions, and it suggests naturalistic analogies to certain traditional religious conceptions, which some may find amusing or thought-provoking."

Although it sounds like a silly argument, it is actually taken at least somewhat seriously in the scientific community. In December of 2016, for example, the topic went viral after numerous news outlets quoted scientist and commentator Neil deGrasse Tyson as saying there was a "very high" chance that the universe is a computer simulation. The question came up at the 2016 Isaac Asimov Memorial Debate, in which a panel was asked whether the universe is a computer simulation.

The question generated a range of answers from the panelists, but deGrasse Tyson, who hosted the debate, said he thought the chances we are living in a simulation "may be very high."

"The question of whether we know that our universe is real has vexed thinkers going far back into history, long before Descartes made his famous 'I think, therefore I am' statement," *Business Insider* notes in a story on the debate.[2] "The same question has been explored in modern science-fiction films like 'The Matrix' and David Cronenberg's 'Existenz.'"\*

During the debate, deGrasse Tyson noted that there could be a much higher intelligence that would make us look like blathering idiots.

"And if that's the case, it is easy for me to imagine that everything in our lives is just the creation of some other entity for their entertainment," Tyson said. "I'm saying, the day we learn that it is true, I will be the only one in the room saying, 'I'm not surprised.'"

He may not be the only one after all. Elon Musk, the

---

\* Not to mention many other films. See the appendix for a list of films and other media which explore ideas related to salvia or the idea of reality as an illusion.

billionaire founder of Tesla Motors, has also reportedly given Bostrom's theory serious thought.³

*The New Yorker*, in an article exploring Bostrom's theory, reported on Musk's answer to a question from a fan about the simulation theory.

"Citing the speed with which video games are improving, he [Musk] suggested that the development of simulations 'indistinguishable from reality' was inevitable. The likelihood that we are living in 'base reality,' he concluded, was just 'one in billions.'"

What of the idea that the universe is holographic, as Peake suggests? It sounds crazy, and yet, it was an idea championed by David Bohm, a brilliant scientist and a protégé of Einstein's. Michael Talbot even wrote a book about the concept, *The Holographic Universe*, which presents an engaging exploration of the idea that we live in a hologram (although a few pseudo-scientific tangents in the book erode Talbot's credibility somewhat).

Media accounts lend further credence to the theory. A *USA Today* story from January 2017 proclaimed, "The entire universe could be a 'vast and complex hologram,' scientists reported Monday. Also, even more unsettling, what we think of as reality may be just an illusion."⁴

The study the story refers to appeared in the journal *Physical Review Letters* and posited that the holographic nature of the universe is akin to 3-D movies: "While we see the pictures as having height, width and depth, they in fact all originate from a flat two dimensional screen," the story states. The authors of the study said they found evidence for the holographic universe after using powerful telescopes to study the Big Bang's "afterglow." The telescopes picked up massive amounts of data within the microwaves left over from the moment of the universe's creation that suggest we may be living in a hologram.

# Philosophy

Peake's and Bostrom's arguments are perfectly interesting philosophical ideas, but it's all pretty much conjecture, right? One could spout off any crazy thing and opine that it's *possible*. That's the basic idea behind the Church of the Flying Spaghetti monster, which, in a critique of organized religion, argues that an invisible flying spaghetti monster exists, despite the lack of evidence that it does. It's a play on "Russell's teapot," the argument* put forth by philosopher Bertrand Russell that the burden of proof lies upon people making unfalsifiable claims, not the people who reject such claims.

My salvia trip, too, can easily be explained away as a hallucination. It's not unusual to hear hippie-types announce that we are all one consciousness, a realization they came to as the result of an LSD-fueled epiphany. I used to dismiss those types of people as crazy. How could you take what you experienced while high on a hallucinogenic drug as some kind of higher truth? And what about the wide variations of hallucinations people have on drugs like LSD? How can all those varying hallucinations be true? Isn't the simplest explanation that under the influence of these drugs, the brain simply makes up a bunch of crazy shit that has no bearing on reality or the nature of the universe?

Likewise, how could I accept my experience on salvia as truth, when it can so easily be dismissed as the result of a foreign substance fucking with the chemicals in my brain?

Here's the difference, though, and I believe it's a profound

---

* Russell wrote, "If I were to suggest that between the Earth and Mars there is a china teapot revolving about the sun in an elliptical orbit, nobody would be able to disprove my assertion provided I were careful to add that the teapot is too small to be revealed even by our most powerful telescopes. But if I were to go on to say that, since my assertion cannot be disproved, it is intolerable presumption on the part of human reason to doubt it, I should rightly be thought to be talking nonsense."

one: Dozens and dozens of people who have used salvia report having what is essentially the *exact same experience*.

To be sure, there are some salvia trip reports that have nothing to do with the illusory nature of reality. But I think there are a number of explanations for that. Some of these are the result of weaker extracts which result in effects that aren't quite as existential-crisis-inducing as the stronger extracts. It's possible that these users didn't go "deep enough" to pull back the illusory curtain obscuring reality's true nature. It's also possible that some people are less able to remember exactly what they experienced.

Whatever is going on, the fact is, most salvia trips are too precisely similar for it to be a mere coincidence. As crazy as it sounds—even to me—I believe that salvia, rather than placing a cloud over the mind, obscuring reality, may actually lift the veil, revealing the true nature of our day-to-day reality. But who knows?

I stumbled across another philosophical argument that seemed to have startling connections with salvia. When I tripped on salvia, there was a distinct sense that the universe was a loop that was unraveling—as if someone were deliberately unspooling a thread and the thread was my perception of reality and of myself.

So when I was browsing a bookstore and saw Douglas Hofstadter's *I Am a Strange Loop*, it caught my attention.

The back of the book declared: "An 'I' is a strange loop where the brain's symbolic and physical levels feed back into each other and flip causality upside down so that symbols seem to have gained the paradoxical ability to push particles around, rather than the reverse.

"To each human being, this 'I' is the realest thing in the world. But how can such a mysterious abstraction be real? Is our

# Philosophy

'I' merely a convenient fiction? Does an 'I' exert genuine power over the particles in our brain, or is it helplessly pushed around by the all-powerful laws of physics?"

One of the things that had been so frightening about my salvia trip was the sense that I had completely lost my "ego," my sense of self, of individuality. I ceased to be a single person, becoming several at once instead. I experienced ego death. So, while Hofstadter's book didn't seem to deal with the nature of the universe and existence, it seemed to deal with the question of the nature of human consciousness in a way that directly related to my experience on salvia.

Hofstadter, a cognition researcher at Indiana University, has a keen interest in the physical processes that make up human consciousness and it is those processes that *I Am a Strange Loop* explores. To be frank, much of the book was way over my head. But it raises an interesting point: If our perception of the universe is tied inexorably to our sense of self, what does it mean about the nature of reality if our sense of self is itself an illusion?

## Anatomy of a Salvia Trip

WHEN I FIRST began researching Salvia, it was people's trip reports that stood out to me the most. The similarities between what they experienced and what I experienced on salvia sent shivers down my spine. But a few particular trip reports caught my attention. One of them, contained in a book that had absolutely nothing to do with salvia, caught me by complete surprise.

For a while, I was an avid reader of books by so-called "pick-up artists," people who believe they have a system for breaking down the social interactions between men and women that can help men seduce women.

One of the books I read on the subject was called *Get Laid or Die Trying: The Field Reports*, by Jeffrey Allen. As I read through it, I almost had a coronary when the author mentioned salvia.

The book, which is a collection of true-life accounts of the author's life, recounts Allen's decision to go to his friend Chrispy's house to smoke salvia.

He doesn't describe whether it was an extract or dried leaves—though, from the description of his experience, it would appear to be the former—but he describes loading it into a bong and taking "two FAT rips" without a second thought, even verbalizing that he didn't think it would do anything.

Within thirty seconds, he was proven wrong.

> I start falling backward through reality, and at the same time reality starts moving forward, like a tunnel. I can't stop it. Everything goes flat, and I become part of it. All of reality is just one thing, one flat-panel picture on a wall or some shit. I can SEE the fourth dimension, time moving, it's like a worm *I'm FUCKED I know I am FUCKING FUCKED* layers keep ripping off reality, like ripping off wrapping paper, and underneath it, it's the same wrapping paper, the layers keep flying off at incredible speed, and there are endless layers, the same thing underneath each one like standing in a roomful of mirrors like one of those computer-generated pictures you see of people where it's made up of little pictures, but imagine the little pictures are all the same image: the big picture and this goes on for infinity, or you pull back from the scene and you keep going, and eventually you see the universe is just an atom in a bigger universe, and when you pull back enough, it's the SAME FUCKING

## Philosophy

SCENE of me sitting there in Chrispy's loft, and THAT universe is an atom in a bigger one that's THE SAME FUCKING THING, over and over again for infinity, I am it and I'm a zipper made out of crayons and I'm being unzipped . . .

I'm not even in the room anymore, it's all gone, it's all flattened out and smeared, all I can see is Chrispy standing there, that's the only thing I can actually discern. Now, I realize, I'm fucking done. My life as I know it is over. I smoked that shit, and it's irrevocably changed everything forever, peeled off the veneer of my life, which was, in fact, not "real" at all. THIS is real. This is it, I'm fucking gone and I'm not coming back. I am incredibly SCARED. My life is OVER. Am I high? I don't remember having taken any drugs. This is REAL and I KNOW I am DONE. My life was all a lie, but it meant something. My whole life was an elaborate joke, or a game. The music on the stereo starts saying shit to me, like literally, it's Creed or Seven Mary Three or something (God knows why he has that shit on) and he starts singing, "You are gone now, dude . . . you are done, it's rotating, you're on the other side . . ." in his Creed voice, which I manage to find somewhat amusing, in spite of everything.

Chrispy isn't Chrispy, he's a construct of the godhead that I can communicate with, like an angel or a demon or a guide from the other side . . . like a fucking David Lynch movie with a supernatural *French midget*. My life has been an illusion that led up to this point where the truth is now revealed, everything that has ever happened in the universe, my childhood, moving here eleven years ago, meeting Chrispy, EVERYTHING, it was all elaborately orchestrated to bring me to this moment. He says, "It's okay, just let it happen," and I'm like, *Fuck, he's known this the entire time I've known him and he never said anything. Now it's over.* It's the creepiest feeling, that everyone was in on the joke but me. They were in on it the whole time, they're just cardboard PROPS in the game. Figments of my imagination. All my friends, my job, all the girls, my whole fucking life was a GAME or maybe a test to train me for the next level, and now it's game over, and I'm transcending to a higher reality. Complexifying into the supercontext. It is immediately clear that my life was like a TV show. It hasn't been real and now I'm being shown that everything I've loved, and everything I've done never really happened. I am terrified and desperate to have my life back, but how can you have something that isn't real? The feeling of loss is so deep and maddening. Literally, I know my life is over and I am dying. So this is what it feels like to die . . . at first I'm struggling and upset that it's all over, thinking about regrets and things I am embarrassed at having done, because God knows I did all that shit, but then, finally, I think, *Fuck it, there's nothing you can do, let's just accept it.* And I just wait for whatever comes next.

"Chrispy," I say.

"Jeffy." I can hear his voice but I'm not sure where it's coming from anymore.

"So," I say tentatively, "what are we gonna do about this?"

"I don't know."

Slowly, however, I start to get an inkling that I can

come back, like if I turn a little, I can become 3-D again. I become aware of the bong in my hand, and I start rotating it . . . it's making the ripping of the layers kind of slow down, and I start to grab on to the 3-D world, and slowly, I come back. It is very surprising when I actually return, more surprising than when I first went "away," in fact.

The whole thing has taken maybe five minutes. Once I'm finally able to make sense of what just happened, I can't stop laughing. "That is the funniest thing I've ever heard in my whole life!" I exclaim to Chrispy. "Man, I thought I was fucked. I thought I was done. This stuff is LEGAL? That's insane. Somebody should do something."

"Haha, yeah I guess."

After about thirty minutes, I feel completely normal. I get up to go, and say goodbye to Chrispy.

"So, that is eet, hah?"

"Yeah, it looks that way."

He slaps me five. "*Bon Voyage.* See you on ze othair side."

Allen's account bears a number of striking similarities to my own experience on salvia. He states that while tripping, "layers keep ripping off reality, like ripping off wrapping paper." I described "riding along several layers of reality that are rapidly peeling away."

Allen also felt that his life was a joke—one that only he was not in on. He states that his friend Chrispy knew the entire time. "It's the creepiest feeling, that everyone was in on the joke but me," he writes. "They were in on it the whole time, they're just

## SUMMER OF SALVIA

cardboard PROPS in the game."

Likewise, I described a fence being lifted like it was "merely a prop in a movie." And everyone seemed to be in on the joke but me—I realized "everyone around me is giggling—giggling at me, amused by my concern, amused by how well they've tricked me into thinking this façade I called reality actually existed."

One thing I had difficulty articulating in my own account of tripping on salvia is the sense of inevitability, and the overwhelming sense of loss at realizing my life was over. Allen, on the other hand, articulates the feeling perfectly.

"I realize, I'm fucking done," he writes. "My life as I know it is over. I smoked that shit, and it's irrevocably changed everything forever . . . I'm fucking gone and I'm not coming back." That's a sentiment shared by countless salvia users, not just Allen and me.

A good example is the book *Salvia Divinorum: Reality of Life and Death*[*] by Stuart Mason. The book appears to be out of print everywhere except Lulu.com—and I didn't have time to order a copy before my deadline for writing this book. But portions of the book are preserved on Google Books,[5] and those portions are adequate to see that Mason's observations of *Salvia divinorum* are eerily similar to my experience, not to mention Jeffrey Allen's.

In the book's introduction, Mason says he first heard of *Salvia divinorum* while researching near-death experiences online. (This is interesting, because Anthony Peake, discussed in the last chapter, is himself a near-death experience researcher, and his research into the near-death experience phenomenon led him to many of the ideas explored in his book, *Is There Life After Death?*)

As I've previously mentioned, I have done salvia a whopping total of one time. I don't intend to ever do it again. Mason, on

---

[*] The book appears to be British, so you'll notice some grammatical peculiarities in the excerpts I've quoted, especially in terms of punctuation.

the other hand, writes that he's experimented with salvia nearly thirty times. His book recounts seventeen of those occasions.

As anyone who has ever seen someone tripping on salvia can attest, people on salvia tend to not make any sense. If they make any noise at all, it's usually gibberish. If they do spit out actual words, they typically make no sense.

Mason, apparently, is an exception to that rule. He writes that he becomes "coherently vocal" while under the influence of salvia. He began recording his sessions in an effort to recall more of his experiences under the drug's effects. While recording oneself would normally prove fruitless for this purpose, Mason's vocal nature apparently made the endeavor worthwhile. After posting the videos online,[6] he discovered that he was far from alone. "To my relief, many people sent me messages saying they had the exact or similar experiences," he writes. "I hadn't gone mad—or at least I wasn't the only one."

Once, under the effects of salvia, Mason found himself in a farmyard setting, with the feeling that he was a small animal. He came across a human-looking man who noticed him and said something to the effect of, "Oh, it's another of your kind again!" Mason got the impression that "our kind" popped up in this other reality from time to time, and were treated as lesser life forms not fully aware of reality.

The farmer picked Mason up by the scruff of his neck and walked him to something that looked like a conveyer belt. He was dropped into a hole in some kind of machinery and was immediately transported back into "consensual reality."†

Mason writes that the experience was colored by an "otherworldly" sensation, not quite sinister, but with the distinct

---

† Mason uses the term "consensual reality" to mean "our everyday, normal reality."

impression that humans were being either kept or looked after by the entities he encountered. The man Mason saw "seemed used to the occurrence and portrayed an attitude similar to that of a farmer tending to escaped livestock," he writes. "Are we being farmed?"

Mason's query as to whether we're some kind of cosmic livestock is interesting, considering that in 2014, media outlets reported on a so-called "Second Livestock Project"*—a proposal to outfit chickens with virtual reality headsets that would give them the impression they were roaming across wide open spaces when they're actually crammed into crowded cages.[7] Though the project was meant more as a thought experiment—there are no plans to actually enact such a livestock program—it's unsettling that the idea is being considered at all. Could it be that in a higher reality, a similar plan was considered and implemented—on us?

Mason notes that the machinery he was plopped into appeared to "either contain our everyday reality, or presented the illusion of it, to whoever was inside." That sounds an awful lot like a virtual reality headset, which projects the illusion of whatever immersive video game one is playing. The difference in Mason's case, however, is that the machinery he saw didn't look high-tech; it looked mechanical, like "some old farm yard contraption."

"It probably might have made more sense if it was computerized or some other futuristic technology, but how can something mechanical as such, create an illusion like the reality we are experiencing right now?" Mason asks.

Mason's description carries a bit of an ominous tone, with the "farmer" sounding like someone hiding the truth from Mason for nefarious purposes. But in a subsequent salvia trip, Mason

---

* "Second Livestock" appears to be a reference to the online game/life simulator "Second Life."

## Philosophy

describes a presence, a female "Being," who he strongly felt was the "mother of my consciousness." He describes a maternal connection that led him to believe that under the effects of salvia, he was transported to his "true home." In addition to the female presence, he said it was apparent that God was his "father."

"My *eternal-mother* told me that, either because God said so, or for my own benefit (I can't be sure), I had to spend more time under the spell of reality/life," he writes. "I did have a distinct feeling that I had exited life prematurely, similar to the anxious feeling of skipping school when you should be in class. I knew I shouldn't be there with her (yet), but the experience was simply too fantastic to willingly surrender."

During my own salvia trip, I remember conversing with an entity and having the same feeling Mason describes—that I was going to return to my life because I wasn't yet ready to leave it. It seemed I was given a choice whether to return to life as Jason Cole, human being, or to stay wherever the hell I found myself after smoking salvia, as whatever the hell I was after smoking salvia.

For Mason, it appeared he had no choice, and he asked his "mother" how much longer he had to stay in "the illusion of Life."

"[I]n a 'mother knows best' loving fashion, she set me down like a baby and covered me with the trail of her long dress—which turned out to be the *fabric* of reality—the illusion of Life. 'Just a little longer. . .' She comforted, as my normal identity came over me with the covering of her dress."

After coming out of the trip, Mason told his sitter he had the impression that we—humanity—had done something "naughty" to be put in our world as a punishment or some kind of corrective measure. "Could consensual reality be a 'correction' facility of some kind?" he asks.

The entirety of Mason's next trip isn't included in the Google Books sample—it starts right in the middle of the trip account—but it's eminently interesting. After entering the "other world" of salvia, he says he became aware that his "real world" self was actually a temporary character he plays in a "game"—implying that life is some kind of cosmic video game, not unlike the Matrix.

Mason said he began telepathically communicating with a Being in the new dimension that told him when he feels like a "person," it is merely "how [he appears] in that game." In the middle of his conversation with the entity, he began describing to his sitter a wheel he had seen that seemed to somehow represent, or even create, our everyday reality.

"You know you can't tell them that!" the entity interjected.

"Why can't I tell them?" he asked. "Does it make a difference if I tell them or not?"

"Still, you can't say it," the being countered.

Mason describes being forbidden to tell of what he'd experienced in this "other dimension." This is similar to my experience, where I told an entity that I vowed "to tell the world about this when I returned." She laughed and said, "Nobody will believe you."

The place Mason goes when he trips on salvia—perhaps the place where all salvia-users go under the drug's effects—seemed to be the place people go when they die, Mason writes. He even asked one of the Beings to "make sure what happens when I die isn't too bad!"

Apparently, in part of the trip account that wasn't included in the preview, one of the Beings told Mason to "Take part in life and just patiently wait till you die to get out."

"But what am I meant to do in the meantime?" Mason asks. "Am I not permitted to know my purpose for being here on earth? I suspect we aren't meant to know until we've actually fulfilled whatever it is that we're supposed to do. Probably, we have more of a chance completing our life's mission without knowing what it is—for if we did, maybe we might refuse to experience it. . .?"

It's a bit chilling to hear Mason talk of death this way in the context of Brett Chidester's suicide. Chidester wrote about life being meaningless. Perhaps he, too, felt there was another dimension where he belonged. Maybe a Being told him to "wait till you die to get out"—and maybe he couldn't wait.

"Maybe we're not meant to remember the structure of reality and how it is cast over the consciousness of man," Mason writes. "If we were to recall how the illusion worked, it might cease to delude us and we'd awaken to our 'real' reality. But so what if we awaken to the real reality? Are we not permitted to be aware of such a truth?"

Mason wonders whether we chose to forget the true nature of reality or were forced into it, but he says he gets a strong sense that his entry to this world was unintentional.

Though Mason describes some frightening experiences on salvia, he nevertheless voices his opposition to efforts to prohibit the drug, writing that it would be a "huge shame" to outlaw Salvia.

"Instead, I believe it deserves credible independent research as evidently, there is a lot that can be learned from it," he writes. "Just the philosophical implications alone warrant serious thought and debate as do the neurological aspects of its influence on our perception of reality."

# Religion

> Everything is meaningless.
> —Ecclesiastes 1:1, Today's New International Version

Entire treatises have been written about each of the world's religions; there's no way I could possibly do a better job—or even a halfway comparable job—of summarizing those religions than the myriad experts who have come before me.

What I intend to do instead is highlight, even if just cursorily, the ways in which tenants of major religions seem to corroborate the salvia experience. Needless to say, the religious implications of tripping on *Salvia divinroum* are staggering.

Imagine growing up and believing your entire life that there was a God watching over you and all of humanity. A God who, for his own divine purposes mysterious and unknown to humankind, crafted the universe with His own hands, created a planet within that universe called Earth, and formed man and woman from its dirt. For someone with such a belief system, the universe may seem vast and mysterious at times, but it is always possible to take solace in the knowledge that, even if you can't possibly know God's plan for your life, there *is* a plan.

Tripping on salvia—for me, at least, but for many other people as well, from what I've read—doesn't leave much room for the possibility of the existence of a God. Or at least, if there is a God or some kind of divine being, it doesn't give a damn about your life. There is no plan for your life. God doesn't give a shit about you. You are not an ant to God—you're a microbe. God doesn't even know you exist.

I must emphasize that when I talk of "doing salvia," I'm talking about smoking potent salvinorin A extract. I've never chewed on the leaves—or smoked them, for that matter—as the Mazatecs do, so I don't know what that's like. All of the online accounts I've found, however, indicate that the experience is considerably milder than the extract, which perhaps accounts for the seeming contradiction of the Catholic, God-fearing Mazatecs partaking in a drug which seems to indicate that God may not exist and, whether or not He does, that human lives are meaningless.

During the panic attack I had while smoking weed several weeks after I'd smoked salvia, I felt like time was repeating itself endlessly. Since then, I've experienced the same thing while smoking weed on at least two other occasions. I've since seen this phenomenon described as *marijuana-induced depersonalization*

# Religion

*disorder.*\* But before then, I didn't know what to call it—I just knew that these were some of the most terrifying experiences of my life.† One thing they did prompt, however, was an exploration of religious ideas besides Christianity (which I was already familiar with) that had alternative ideas of the universe—such as that the universe and time are cyclical.

Sometimes the idea of a cyclical universe in religions is metaphorical. The idea is that the universe goes through "seasons," even as time travels down a linear path.

But some religions believe the universe literally repeats itself, over and over, for all eternity. This is an idea known as *eternal recurrence* or *eternal return*, as I found out after somehow ending up on the Wikipedia page explaining the concept. It sounds eerily similar to Anthony Peake's assertion that we relive our lives over and over, perhaps in the hope of learning some great lesson or righting some wrong that has been playing out for eons.

---

\* Depersonalization disorder, also known as depersonalization-derealization syndrome, is associated with dissociative disorders. The Diagnostic and Statistical Manual of Mental Disorders says the diagnostic criteria for the disorder include "longstanding or recurring feelings of being detached from one's mental processes or body, as if one is observing them from the outside or in a dream," as well as "derealization, experiencing the external world as strange or unreal," and "a sense that other people seem unfamiliar or mechanical." It also stipulates that for an official diagnosis, the depersonalization "is not associated with substance use or a medical illness." Though my depersonalization was induced by marijuana, it continued long after the effects of the marijuana had worn off. And though I was never formally diagnosed with depersonalization disorder, it seemed to perfectly describe my symptoms after my marijuana-induced panic attacks. I was plagued by a feeling of unreality—like I didn't exist—that persisted for weeks, if not months.

† I'm not the only one. For example, on an online forum, a nineteen-year-old said that after suffering from marijuana-induced depersonalization, "The environment feels fake and my memory and concentration is non existent [sic]. I do not have any symptoms of physical anxiety but rather my perception of the world is distorted." To read the original post, go to: bluelight.org/vb/threads/625404-How-long-does-Cannabis-induced-Derealization-last

The idea of eternal recurrence can be found in many religions and philosophies, including eastern religions such as Hinduism or Buddhism, and even Judaism.

In Indian religions, for example, the concept of the "wheel of life"[1] represents "an endless cycle of birth, life, and death from which one seeks liberation." Tantric Buddhism boasts a "wheel of time," known as the *Kalachakra*, which "expresses the idea of an endless cycle of existence and knowledge."

In the Hindu scripture called the *Bhagavad Gita*, Hindu deity Krishna describes the "repeating nature of universe."

"Knowing that thousand eras constitute a day of *Brahman*, [and] thousand eras complete a night,\* are the people who know day, [and] night. On arrival of day, all manifestations originate from 'Unmanifest'; On arrival of night they annihilate into [what is] known as 'Unmanifest' only. This [same] elementary world only happens again and again; Annihilates upon arrival of night, [and] originates upon arrival of day."

The notion can also be found in Judaism, which posits a cyclical concept of time for those in the physical world, although the Creator is eternal and exists outside of time. The cyclical concept of time found in Judaism, however, seems to be more figurative than in eastern religions.

More evidence of eternal recurrence's prominence in human history is the *Ouroboros*, a symbol represented as a snake or dragon devouring its own tail.

Physician-philosopher Sir Thomas Browne reportedly tied the symbol to eternal recurrence in a letter to a friend in 1657:

---

\* It's interesting to note that a similar line can be found in the Christian Bible. The line that a "thousand eras constitute a day of *Brahman*" echoes 2 Peter 3:8-9, which states that, "With the Lord a day is like a thousand years, and a thousand years are like a day."

# Religion

"that the first day should make the last, that the Tail of the Snake should return into its Mouth precisely at that time, and they should wind up upon the day of their Nativity, is indeed a remarkable Coincidence, which tho Astrology hath taken witty pains to salve, yet hath it been very wary in making Predictions of it." Browne's *The Garden of Cyrus* also makes mention of eternal recurrence: "All things began in order, so shall they end, and so shall they begin again."

Though the idea of eternal recurrence may seem somewhat farfetched to our modern way of thinking, it actually has analogues in modern scientific theories.

Most people are familiar with the "big bang theory"—the theory that our universe was once concentrated into a single, infinitely small point, which suddenly exploded in a "big bang," sending the universe outward at a rapid rate of expansion. Fewer people are aware of the concept of the "big crunch."

The big crunch is part of the "oscillating universe" theory, which posits that the universe will collapse on itself in a "big crunch," with all of the matter and energy in the universe once again condensed into a single point, before erupting once again in a big bang, followed by a big crunch, which will then be followed by another big bang . . . and so on, for infinity. Sounds a lot like "eternal recurrence" on a universal scale, doesn't it?

The theory dates back to the 1930s, with cosmologists such as Professor Alexander Vilenkin from Tufts University, and Professor Max Tegmark of the Massachusetts Institute of Technology.

According to Wikipedia, these men's work suggests that "if space is sufficiently large and uniform, or infinite as some theories suggest, and if quantum theory is true such that there is only a finite number of configurations within a finite volume possible, due to Heisenberg's uncertainty principle, then identical instances of the history of Earth's entire Hubble volume* occur every so often, *simply by chance*."

German philosopher Friedrich Nietzsche often explored the ramifications of cyclical time in his writing.

In *The Gay Science*, Nietzsche reflects on the concept of eternal recurrence, posing the following scenario: "What, if some day or night a demon were to steal after you into your loneliest loneliness and say to you: 'This life as you now live it and have lived it, you will have to live once more and innumerable times more'. . . Would you not throw yourself down and gnash your teeth and curse the demon who spoke thus? Or have you once experienced a tremendous moment when you would have answered him: 'You are a god and never have I heard anything more divine.'"

The idea fits into Nietzsche's concept of *amor fati*, or "love of fate," the idea that one must fully accept their fate, embracing the way their life unfolds—both the good and the bad. "My formula for human greatness is *amor fati*: that one wants to have nothing different, not forward, not backward, not in all eternity," Nietzsche writes. "Not merely to bear the necessary, still less to conceal it—all idealism is mendaciousness before the necessary—but to *love* it."

I think it would be absolutely divine to be afforded an opportunity to go back and live my life again—as long as I were given the opportunity to remedy all the mistakes and wrong turns I've made. But the thought of living my life again exactly as I've already lived it, repeating the same mistakes over and over again, is horrific. I definitely wouldn't be praising Nietzsche's demon as a god. On the other hand, I wouldn't exactly curse the demon, either. For all the mistakes I've made in my life, I've also lived

---

* A Hubble volume, according to Wikipedia, is a "spherical region of the Universe surrounding an observer beyond which objects recede from that observer at a rate greater than the speed of light due to the expansion of the Universe."

many immeasurably joyful moments. If I were to relive my life, never realizing I wasn't living it for the first time, the bad and good moments would balance out, I think.

But that's the rub: With salvia, it's like the veil is lifted and you glimpse the truth. This plant, touched by the divine, reveals to you the cyclical nature of your life. Once that veil has been lifted, it's impossible to simply carry on with your life the same as before.

It is not uncommon for salvia users to experience this same sense that their life is stuck on repeat. Take, for instance, an account posted by an anonymous user to Salvia-trip.net titled, "Does my life repeat."[2]

The user—we'll assume they're a male to simplify the pronouns used in this account—states that he hates tripping on salvia because, "I realize that my whole life is just some scripted repeating hell that I am stuck in for all of eternity. I remembered all of the other millions of times I have lived my life and I remembered what will happen in the trip from the other countless times I have lived through it."

Part of this eternal script, he felt, was that while tripping on salvia, he would never be able to leave his room, because he was not meant to. The only way to break the script and end the ever-repeating hell was for him to leave his room, "thus causing me to break free from my scripted reality."

But he remembered already trying to break free millions of times before, to no avail, as his sitter always prevented him from leaving. Confirming his suspicions, he tried to leave, but was stopped by his sitter, causing him great stress as he realized he would never break free of the endless cycle.

"No matter what, the next time I live my life, I will never be able to open the door, Its [sic] not in my script to open the door, so I never will," he writes. "This trip permanently changed the way

I view life, as I realized that I will never end this hell of repeating the same exact life over and over and over again. There is no afterlife for me, only this. I have typed this message to you a million times, and will do it a million times more."

IN EASTERN RELIGIONS, including Hinduism and Buddhism, it is taught that existence is an illusion, *maya*. According to the *Encyclopedia Brittanica*, *maya* originally referred to the "magic power" that allowed gods to trick human beings into believing some kind of illusion was true.[3] But it also came to refer to an illusion at a more basic level, referring to "the powerful force that creates the cosmic illusion that the phenomenal world is real . . . Maya is reflected on the individual level by human ignorance (*ajnana*) of the real nature of the self, which is mistaken for the empirical ego but which is in reality identical with *brahman*."*

Swami Vivekananda, an Indian Hindu monk who helped introduce Hinduism to the Western world in the 1800s, wrote that Vedic literature—sacred Hindu texts—refers to the idea of *maya* as "delusion."

Though it doesn't mention *maya* by name, the question is asked in the Hindu scriptures, "Why can't we know this secret of the universe?" The answer that was given was, "Because we talk in vain, and because we are satisfied with the things of the senses, and because we are running after desires; therefore, we, as it were, cover the Reality with a mist."

"We get the idea," Vivekananda writes, "that the cause of our ignorance is a kind of mist that has come between us and the Truth."

---

* Brahman, in Hinduism, is "the ultimate reality underlying all phenomena."

# Religion

Vivekananda goes on to write that "delusion" or "illusion" is an inadequate definition of *maya*, and to be sure, there is debate about exactly what is meant by "illusion." But what is clear is that the adherents of this ancient religion believed a divine presence had the ability to obscure the true nature of reality.

This idea that "because we are running after desires," some deity has decided to "cover the Reality with a mist," is an important connection to salvia. Although the mist could be seen figuratively, as a love for material pleasures that distracts from a thirst for the divine, one could also interpret it more literally. Taken that way, it sounds a lot like the truth revealed by salvia.

As I've mentioned in earlier chapters, while tripping on salvia, I seemed to have a choice whether to stay in "salvia space," or return to—for lack of a better term—the "real" world. And I may have chosen wrong. It's almost like whatever entity I was interacting with wanted me to learn to forget the material pleasures of this world, to accept their impermanence and unimportance. But I couldn't. I wasn't done living my life.

The idea that we generate a "mist" that obscures reality also reminds me of Stuart Mason's description of the trail of his "mother's" dress forming the "fabric of reality."† The dress, like the

---

† The subtitle for this book is, "Exploring nature's most powerful hallucinogen and the fabric of existence." This phrase, "fabric of existence," and the similar "fabric of reality," come up frequently when reading about salvia. Here are two prominent examples: When Daniel Siebert first tripped on salvia, he wrote immediately afterward that the drug was "tearing apart the fabric of existence. It is madness." Stuart Mason also uses the phrase in describing the dress of a salvia-related entity, saying, "she set me down like a baby and covered me with the trail of her long dress—which turned out to be the *fabric* of reality—the illusion of Life." (Emphasis in the original text). Can it be a mere coincidence that two separate users of salvia used language so precisely identical when describing their respective salvia trips? Perhaps, but I think it's also possible that they used similar language because they shared the exact same experience, so it was natural for them to use the same words to describe it.

mist, generates a façade we call "reality," when in fact, the true nature of existence is hidden beneath it.

Speaking of the true nature of existence, let's talk a little (or a lot) about Philip K. Dick.

Dick was a science fiction author who lived from 1928 to 1982. Hollywood has made several films based on his books and short stories, including *Blade Runner*, *Total Recall*, *Minority Report*, and *A Scanner Darkly*.

Beginning in 1984, Dick had a kind of religious experience, in which he believed a higher power essentially beamed information about the nature of reality into his brain. There are many accounts describing this experience,* but one of the most entertaining is in the form of a comic by cartoonist Robert Crumb.[4]

The information in Crumb's comic is taken from a 1981 interview Dick gave with Gregg Rickman. The comic introduces Dick as an author whose books "often dealt with the illusory quality of reality as we know it." That's a bit of an understatement. But it's certainly no mistake that we're discussing Dick in a book that's all about the "illusory quality of reality" as revealed by *Salvia divinorum*.

Anyway, here's how Dick's eye-opening, mystic experience went down, as recounted by Crumb:

In March 1974, at his home in Fullerton, California, Dick sat in excruciating pain after having a wisdom tooth removed. The dentist had given him a large dose of sodium pentothal—the drug traditionally depicted as a "truth serum" in popular culture—but had not sent him home with any pain medication.

---

* Including an entire book on Philip K. Dick by Anthony Peake, titled, *A Life of Philip K. Dick: The Man Who Remembered the Future*.

# Religion

Dick's wife called the pharmacy, which sent a young woman to deliver the medication to his home.

Dick answered the door when the woman arrived. He noticed a fish necklace dangling from her neck. The sun struck the necklace, and the glare shone into Dick's eyes—he was "dazed by it," he said.

Everything else, including his pain, seemed to fade into the background and he couldn't stop staring at the necklace. Dick asked the girl what the fish symbol meant, and she explained it was a symbol used by the early Christians.

"In that instant," Dick remembered, "as I stared at the gleaming fish sign and heard her words, I suddenly experienced what I later learned is called *anamnesis*—a Greek word meaning, literally, 'loss of forgetfulness.' I remembered who I was and where I was. In an instant, in the twinkling of an eye, it all came back to me. And not only could I remember it but I could see it. The girl was a secret Christian and so was I. We lived in fear of detection by the Romans. We had to communicate in cryptic signs. She had just told me all this and it was true. I saw the world as the world of the apostolic Christian times of ancient Rome, when the fish sign was in use."

For the next year, Dick says he perceived this ancient Christian world beneath his everyday existence. He states that it was "an eternal truth, like Plato's archetypical world, where everything was always here and always now, and had been that way and would be that way."

Then, one day, Dick was sitting in his home, eyes closed, listening to "Strawberry Fields Forever" by the Beatles,[†] when he was suddenly hit by a "tremendous light."

---

[†] Which, eerily enough, contains the lyrics, "Nothing is real."

"I was blinded," he said. "I thought, Jesus Christ! What's happening? I'm blind, my head hurts, can't see nothing. All I can see is pink . . . a phosphene after image, like you see when a flashbulb fires off."

The words of the song he was listening to changed, and delivered a message that his young son, Christopher, was in mortal danger. His wife took their son to the hospital, where the doctors informed her that Christopher needed life-saving surgery immediately. According to Dick, that was only one of the miraculous things that occurred after his encounter with the pink light.

Though Dick had trouble interpreting what happened to him, he summed it up by saying, "I just know that some kind of spirit took me over . . . through its help I was able to solve problems and concerns, the things I couldn't do . . . it seemed able to discern anything I looked at."

Dick kept a journal in which he tried to make sense of what he believed was the divine knowledge that had been transmitted into his mind. He called this journal his *exegesis*, and a large portion of it was published in 2011.[5] Dick's exegesis touches upon Gnosticism often. In fact, he came to consider himself, somewhat reluctantly, a gnostic.

What is Gnosticism? In his exegesis, Dick offers the following list explaining what he believes to be the "ten major principles of the Gnostic revelation":[6]

> 1. The creator of this world is demented.
> 2. The world is not as it appears, in order to hide the evil in it, a delusive veil obscuring it and the deranged deity.
> 3. There is another, better realm of God, and all our efforts are to be directed toward

## Religion

a. returning there

b. bringing it here.

4. Our actual lives stretch thousands of years back, and we can be made to remember our origin in the stars.

5. Each of us has a divine counterpart unfallen who can reach a hand down to us to awaken us. This other personality is the authentic waking self, the one we have now is asleep and minor.\* We are in fact asleep, and in the hands of a dangerous magician disguised as a good god, the deranged creator deity. The bleakness, the evil and pain in this world, the fact that it is a deterministic prison controlled by a demented creator causes us willingly to split with the reality principle early in life, and so to speak willingly fall asleep in delusion.

6. You can pass from the delusional prison world into the Peaceful kingdom *if* the True Good God places you under His grace and allows you to see reality through His eyes.

7. Christ gave, rather than received, revelation; he taught his followers how to enter the kingdom *while still alive*, where other mystery religions only bring about anamnesis: knowledge of it as the "other time" in "the other realm," not here. He causes it to come here, and is the living agency of the Sole Good God (i.e. the Logos).

8. Probably the real, secret Christian church still exists, long underground, with the living Corpus Christi as its head or ruler, the members absorbed into it. Through

---

\* This sounds remarkably similar to the *Daemon* described by Anthony Peake. On the back of his book *The Daemon: A Guide to Your Extraordinary Secret Self*, Peake contends that, "all consciously aware beings consist of not one but two separate consciousnesses: everyday consciousness and that of the Daemon, a higher being that seems to possess knowledge of future events."

participation in it they probably have vast, seemingly magical powers.

9. The division into "two times" (good and evil) and "two realms" (good and evil) will abruptly end with victory for the good time here, as the presently invisible kingdom separates and becomes visible. We cannot know the date.

10. During this time period we are on the sifting bridge being judged according to which power we give allegiance to, the deranged creator demiurge of this world or the One Good God and his kingdom, whom we know through Christ.

Dick adds ominously that, "To know these ten principles of gnostic Christianity is to court disaster."

The exact tenants of Gnosticism vary according to different sects and religious bents, each iteration involving a different set of terminology and cast of characters. I'm not going to get into all of them (though it's all very interesting and worth looking into). One common thread, however, is the idea that our everyday reality is the illusory product of a demented, less-than-all-powerful God known as the *Demiurge.*

According to at least some Gnostic texts, the physical world was ultimately brought into existence through the actions of Sophia, a god-like figure who, according to some Gnostic accounts, was an equal partner or spouse to God.[7] Her desire to become closer to God led to her getting kicked out of heaven—not unlike Eve's taste of the forbidden fruit leading to her and Adam's exile from Eden. Upon her banishment from heaven, Sophia gave birth to the Demiurge, a deranged, god-like creature which Gnostics believe to be the God of the Old Testament.

# Religion

Gnostics consider this incarnation of God evil and, further, less powerful than the true, all-powerful God. Gnostics believe that because the Demiurge is evil, the material world is also evil. The only way to escape the physical world is through *gnosis*, or knowledge. Jesus Christ was considered a messenger of this redeeming knowledge.

Dick's interest in Gnosticism is apparent throughout his body of work, but it is perhaps most evident in his semi-autobiographical novel *VALIS*.

In *VALIS*, a character based on Dick develops what he calls a "two source cosmogony"—an explanation of "how the cosmos came into existence."

It goes like this:[8]

> The One was and was-not, combined, and desired to separate the was-not from the was. So it generated a diploid* sac which contained, like an eggshell, a pair of twins, each an androgyny, spinning in opposite directions (the Yin and Yang of Taoism, with the One as the Tao). The plan of the One was that both twins would emerge into being (wasness) simultaneously; however, motivated by a desire to be (which the One had implanted in both twins), the counter-clockwise twin broke through the sac and separated prematurely; i.e., before full term. This was the dark or Yin twin. Therefore it was defective. At full term the wiser twin emerged. Each twin formed a unitary entelechy, a single living organism made of *psyche* and *soma*, still rotating in opposite directions to each

---

* From Wiktionary.com: "Of a cell, having a pair of each type of chromosome, one of the pair being derived from the ovum and the other from the spermatozoon. Most somatic cells of higher organisms are diploid."

other. The full term twin, called Form I by Parmenides,* advanced correctly through its growth stages, but the prematurely born twin, called Form II, languished.

The next step in the One's plan was that the Two would become the Many, through their dialectic interaction. From them as hyperuniverses they projected a hologram-like interface, which is the pluriform universe we creatures inhabit. The two sources were to intermingle equally in maintaining our universe, but Form II continued to languish toward illness, madness and disorder. These aspects she projected into our universe.

It was the One's purpose for our holographic universe to serve as a teaching instrument by which a variety of new lives advanced until ultimately they would be isomorphic† with the One. However, the decaying condition of hyperuniverse II introduced malfactors which damaged our hologramatic universe. This is the origin of entropy, undeserved suffering, chaos and death, as well as the Empire, the Black Iron Prison; in essence, the aborting of the proper health and growth of the life forms within the hologramatic universe. Also the teaching function was grossly impaired, since only the signal from the hyperuniverse I was information-rich; that from II had become noise.

The psyche of hyperuniverse I sent a micro-form of itself into hyperuniverse II to attempt to heal it. The

---

* Again, from Wiktionary.com: "An Ancient Greek philosopher born in Elea, in southern Italy. Founder of the Eleatic school of philosophy."

† Gee, I sure rely on Wiktionary.com a lot, don't I? They define "isomorphic" as, "Having a similar structure or function to something that is not related genetically or through evolution."

microform was apparent in our hologramatic universe as Jesus Christ. However, hyperuniverse II, being deranged, at once tormented, humiliated, rejected and finally killed the micro-form of the healing *psyche* of her healthy twin. After that, hyperuniverse II continued to decay into blind, mechanical, purposeless causal processes. It then became the task of Christ (more properly the Holy Spirit) to either rescue the life forms in the hologramatic universe, or abolish all influences on it emanating from II. Approaching its task with caution, it prepared to kill the deranged twin, since she cannot be healed; i.e., she will not allow herself to be healed because she does not understand that she is sick. This illness and madness pervades us and makes us idiots living in private, unreal worlds. The original plan of the One can only be realized now by the division of hyperuniverse I into two healthy hyperuniverses, which will transform the hologramatic universe into the successful teaching machine it was designed to be. We will experience this as the "Kingdom of God."

Within time, hyperuniverse II remains alive: "The Empire never ended." But in eternity, where the hyperuniverses exist, she has been killed—of necessity—by the healthy twin of hyperuniverse I, who is our champion. The One grieves for this death, since the One loved both twins; therefore the information of the Mind consists of a tragic tale of the death of a woman, the undertones of which generate anguish into all the creatures of the hologramatic universe without their knowing why. This grief will depart when the healthy twin undergoes mitosis* and the "Kingdom of God" arrives. The machinery for this transformation—the procession within time from the Age of Iron to the Age of Gold—is at work now; in eternity it is already accomplished.

The Gnostic philosophy—and Dick's interpretation of it in particular—is the most markedly similar to the salvia experience of any religion or philosophy, in my opinion. Consider the contention that the universe as we know it is illusory, that there is a real, spiritual universe just beyond our reach. In Dick's "principles of Gnostic revelation," he writes that, "The world is not as it appears, in order to hide the evil in it, a delusive veil obscuring it and the deranged deity."

The idea of a veil obscuring the true nature of reality is one that permeates the salvia experience. It's not just that reality is illusory; it's the fact that the illusory reality has been created in a concerted effort to conceal the true nature of reality from us. Think of Stuart Mason's "mother" figure draping the trail of her dress over him and sending him back into "consensual reality."

Whatever your interest in science fiction, it's difficult not to think that Philip K. Dick was onto something.

---

* Wiktionary.com: "The division of a cell nucleus in which the genome is copied and separated into two identical halves. It is normally followed by cell division."

# Conclusions

> Psychedelics are illegal not because a loving government is concerned that you may jump out of a third story window. Psychedelics are illegal because they dissolve opinion structures and culturally laid down models of behavior and information processing. They open you up to the possibility that everything you know is wrong.
> —Terence Mckenna

I'VE GATHERED INFORMATION ABOUT MANY IDEAS RELATED TO *Salvia divinorum* in this book. But what does all that information mean? What is the point of a salvia trip? Is there one?

To answer that question, I think it's necessary to sift through peoples' various experiences on salvia—as well as some other philosophical and religious ideas—and see how they're all tied together. I've also included some salvia trip reports that haven't been quoted thus far in the book. Consider the following points:

## Summer of Salvia

### One: Reality Isn't Real.

If there's one takeaway from experiencing a salvia trip, it's that reality isn't real. It's an illusion. Just ask:

**Jason Cole:** "As the spinning and pulling continue, my perspective shifts and I'm riding along several layers of reality that are rapidly peeling away, one right after the other as if someone's peeling off a potato's skin, except once they peel one layer of skin, there's another beneath it, so they repeat the process again and again. Each layer is a level of illusion. Each layer has been carefully placed on top of the other to conceal the true nature of reality. Each layer is a deception, a dream, a mask. A little more truth is revealed with each one's removal. The truth becomes clearer and as it does I grow more and more apprehensive."

**Daniel Siebert:** "At some point I realized that what I was trying to get back to did not exist—it was just an ephemeral dream. . . . TEARING APART THE FABRIC OF REALITY. This is tooooooooo strong. It is tearing apart the fabric of existence. It is madness. Thank god it only lasted 10-15 minutes!"

**Jeffrey Allen:** "All of reality is just one thing, one flat-panel picture on a wall or some shit. I can SEE the fourth dimension, time moving, it's like a worm *I'm FUCKED I know I am FUCKING FUCKED* layers keep ripping off reality, like ripping off wrapping paper, and underneath it, it's the same wrapping paper, the layers keep flying off at incredible speed, and there are endless layers."

**Brett Chidester:** "Salvia makes me realize that humans have no reason to be on Earth. We are all just grains of sand on reality beach."

**Stuart Mason:** "[I]n a 'mother knows best' loving fashion, she set me down like a baby and covered me with the trail of her

## Conclusions

long dress—which turned out to be the *fabric* of reality—the illusion of Life. 'Just a little longer. . .' She comforted, as my normal identity came over me with the covering of her dress."

### Two: The True Nature of Reality is Being Purposely Hidden

The second truth suggested by salvia is that our illusory reality is actually masking the true nature of our existence:

**Jason Cole:** "Each layer is a level of illusion. Each layer has been carefully placed on top of the other to conceal the true nature of reality. Each layer is a deception, a dream, a mask."

**Jeffrey Allen:** "Now, I realize, I'm fucking done. My life as I know it is over. I smoked that shit, and it's irrevocably changed everything forever, peeled off the veneer of my life, which was, in fact, not 'real' at all. THIS is real. This is it, I'm fucking gone and I'm not coming back."

**Philip K. Dick:** "The world is not as it appears, in order to hide the evil in it, a delusive veil obscuring it and the deranged deity."

**Swami Vivekananda:** "We get the idea that the cause of our ignorance is a kind of mist that has come between us and the Truth."

### Three: Life is a Joke

One of the trademarks of the YouTube videos depicting salvia trips is that the users often erupt in a fit of hysterical laughter. What are they laughing at? Their life—because it's nothing more than a cosmic joke:

**Jason Cole:** "I look to my left at a wood picket fence surrounding the perimeter of the yard and suddenly a group of construction workers appears from nowhere and easily lifts the fence as if it were merely a prop in a movie, as if they've been asked to come dismantle the set. They walk off, laughing, and I realize everyone around me is giggling—giggling at me, amused by my concern, amused by how well they've tricked me into thinking this facade I called reality actually existed."

**Jeffrey Allen:** "My life was all a lie, but it meant something. My whole life was an elaborate joke, or a game. . . . It's the creepiest feeling, that everyone was in on the joke but me. They were in on it the whole time, they're just cardboard PROPS in the game. Figments of my imagination. All my friends, my job, all the girls, my whole fucking life was a GAME or maybe a test to train me for the next level, and now it's game over, and I'm transcending to a higher reality."

**1248853, posting on Reddit:**[1] "Everything begins to laugh at me as if wow you Finally realized. i am taken behind the scenes of reality. my family and friends and material possessions being the actors. Strong resemblance to the truman show . . ."

### Four: Your Ego Shatters; You Desperately Cling to Your Life:

Who are you? It doesn't matter, because when you take salvia, you not only lose your ego, your identity—you realize it never existed in the first place.

**Jason Cole:** "A small piece of my ego peels away with each layer. I try to grasp these fleeing fragments of my essence, but they slide through my mental fingers and I realize it's hopeless.

## Conclusions

My self slowly fades and even though I am still somehow aware, it is without the benefit of an ego."

**Daniel Siebert:** "At this point I realized that I had no actual memory of ever having existed in any other state of consciousness than the disembodied one I was now in."

**1248853, posting on Reddit:** "The first thing that happens is, all matter becomes consciousness, it is part of me but i am no longer insert name. I am just. There is no differentiation between my awareness, and the physical make up of my walls, or guitar. . . . Then, the fear comes in after this realization that I am stuck in a space of pure 'just'. i cannot comprehend this, it doesn't make sense."

### Five: When the True Nature of Reality is Revealed, You're Dragged in a Specific Direction

I don't know what it means, but numerous salvia trip reports make mention of the user being dragged in a specific direction. I'm not sure how to interpret this, but it's noteworthy that so many people independently report this experience.

**Jason Cole:** "Everything drags down and to the right. It's not just me—the entire universe is being pulled into a vortex in the corner of some impossibly gargantuan room. Down and to the right, down and to the right, inevitably, irrevocably, and as much as I try to resist it, the pull is unavoidable."

**Fantasticfungus, posting on Shroomery.com:**[2] "Lots of people describe salvias physical pulling effect to the right, most people are right handed of course, so have any 'cagy-handed' salvia tripper's noticed being spun round to the left ?"

**Anonymous Report on Salvia-trip.net:**[3] "Outside, I felt like

I was being strongly pulled (not pushed) in a direction approximately northerly... The pull now became an enormously strong downward pull, I felt like had my feet not been on the floor I would just spin forwards. Sounds became distorted. I felt the downwards pull on my neck, my jaw, and then my eyes. That's when my vision decided to follow the pull. Suddenly everything in my vision blurred vertically, as if I was really spinning round and round, going head over heels over and over again at great speed. At this point, my mouth was open, my head was forward and my chin was touching the top of my chest. I just couldn't resist the pull."

**Hubert Cumberdale, posting on Erowid:**[4] "I felt gravity's pull, but it was pulling me sideways. I felt an extremely strong tug downward, and this intensified as the trip became more and more intense."

## Six: There Are Alien or Supernatural Entities in the True Reality

Salvia trip reports are rife with descriptions of encounters with alien entities. Whether these creatures are from another dimension or are divine representatives—angels, or even gods (or, for that matter, demons) is unclear. Of particular note is that many people report seeing a female entity known as "Lady Salvia." The entity I spoke with seemed to have a female persona, as did the "mother" Stuart Mason encountered.

**Jason Cole:** "That chorus reverberates throughout the entire trip and suddenly it's not the dark-skinned girl saying it, it's some unearthly presence. I can't tell if it's a woman or some genderless, entirely inhuman creature."

## Conclusions

**Stuart Mason:** "But in a subsequent salvia trip, Mason describes a presence, a female 'Being,' who he strongly felt was the 'mother of my consciousness.' He describes a maternal connection that led him to believe that under the effects of salvia, he was transported to his 'true home.' In addition to the female presence, he said it was apparent that God was his 'father.'"

**Tranced, posting on Bluelight.org:**[5] "An utterly beautiful fractal goddess made from the colours of gold, green and autumn leaves. She looked young, maybe around 18 years old, and I got the undeniable feeling that I knew her from somewhere. Not only in terms of being a familiar face, but in terms of being a distinctive, powerful, female archetype. It was like her face cycled through the face of every human female who had ever lived."

### Seven: We Visit the "True" Reality Over and Over Again

One of the most overwhelming feelings permeating the salvia experience is the sensation that this is not the first time you've visited this other dimension. It feels like you've been there more times than you could possibly count.

**Jason Cole:** "Yet there's a familiarity to her, to all of this, as if I've experienced this exact scenario millions of times before. No, not millions—that figure is woefully inadequate. . . . I vow to tell the world about this when I return and she laughs. Nobody will believe you, she explains. How do you know? I ask. Because this has been happening for eons, she replies. This journey is antediluvian, as old as anything in or outside of the universe."

**Stuart Mason:** "Once, under the effects of salvia, Mason found himself in a farmyard setting, with the feeling that he was a small animal. He came across a human-looking man who noticed him and said something to the effect of, 'Oh, it's another of your kind again!' Mason got the impression that 'our kind' popped up in this other reality from time to time, and were treated as lesser life forms not fully aware of reality."

**Hubert Cumberdale, posting on Erowid:** "I felt the most intense feeling of déjà vu as all sense of self died. I had been here before! Now why the fuck would I ever return? The idea of taking this drug recreationally seemed as naïve, foolish, and immature as anything you could ever imagine."

THERE ARE MORE similarities than I could possibly count; these are simply the ones that jump out at me as the most significant. But I could go on forever.

Take the "wheel" that Stuart Mason experienced on his salvia trip, which seemed to generate our reality: "After a period of silence, I turned to my sitter in an attempt to explain what I had seen and experienced," he writes. "I had started to describe the wheel and how it represented our reality."

It bears an uncanny reseblance to an account on Erowid. A user named Vulpine penned a trip report titled, "Reality is a Five-Spoked Wheel."[6]

"I was a five-pointed wheel," they write. "Reality itself was the five-spoked wheel. . . . I was actually a consciousness inside the tumbling object, rotating in it's [sic] chambers while aware of all the chambers. They were full of light and beautifully riotous colors. As I tumbled in my colorful bucket, through an opening in my chamber I could sometimes see out into another world, the base or real reality. . . . I became cognizant that my entire life, or what I had perceived it to be, all 27 years, were actually an illusion. They were merely a fancy I had generated while

## Conclusions

watching the interplay of light, color, and shadow in my bucket. Any minute now I would be tumbled out onto the grass, forever lost from this false, comfortable reality and loosed into the base reality outside, forever cut off from the illusion of my life I was used too [sic]."

Not only do we have an account corroborating Mason's description of a wheeled object generating or projecting our "consensual reality," we also have another user realizing, through the power of salvia, that their entire life has been a lie, an illusion. Their realization sounds almost exactly like the ones experienced by me, by Jeffrey Allen, and by countless other people not mentioned in this book.

So just what in the hell is going on? Are these similarities a coincidence? Are they inconsequential?

I suppose you could say it's no different than any other drug producing a similar effect among its users. Alcohol makes countless people throw up. Marijuana frequently causes panic attacks. Ibuprofen relieves aches and pains. Yet, we don't find it remarkable or spine-tingling that people have common experiences on these drugs.

It's also not uncommon for hallucinogens to engender seemingly-profound revelations. Just look at the seventies in its entirety—look at post-LSD Beetles music.

Here's the thing that I find troubling, though. Sure, LSD causes people to reach similar conclusions about, say, the interconnectedness of humanity or the existence of other dimensions that we can't perceive with our everyday senses.

But to my knowledge, no other drug (with the possible exception of DMT), regularly engenders such strikingly similar hallucinations to such a narrow degree.

I wholeheartedly admit that confirmation bias could be

contributing to this conclusion. I've gone out of my way to find accounts of salvia trips that corroborate my own trip, and have put little effort into collecting counterexamples.

It is true that plenty of salvia trips have nothing to do with startling revelations about reality as an illusion. Likewise, there are plenty that do not involve interacting with supernatural beings, or any of the other ideas explored in this book. At the same time, I could offer numerous explanations for why this is. For one, it could be that every salvia trip *is* the same, but not everyone is able to recall every aspect of their trip. So even if someone does realize that reality is an illusion during their trip, by the time the drug's effects have worn off, they've forgotten that aspect in favor of some other detail—whether it's melting into the couch, becoming a shoe, or whatever.

It's also possible that a variety of factors influence what kind of trip one experiences. It's almost like the entities on the other side choose who gets the "real" experience and who gets some kind of false, decoy experience because they're not ready for the truth, or because they aren't giving the drug its proper respect (which doesn't quite make sense, since—just to name two examples—neither Jeffrey Allen or myself went into the experience with any degree of reverence, yet still had profound experiences that suggested reality is an illusion).

I wrote this book searching for answers to questions. But after years of research and pondering, it appears I may have only reached one conclusion with any certainty: My search for the truth is futile.

# Epilogue: Truth

> The truth belongs to God. The mistakes were mine.
> —MEWITHOUTYOU, "In a Market Dimly Lit"

I STARTED WRITING THIS BOOK AROUND 2009, MAYBE 2010. It's taken me seven years to finish writing it. Life gets busy.

At one time, I had planned to make this book a chronicle of my life up to the point of publication. But a lot has happened in seven years.

To summarize, I graduated from college and lost touch with many of the characters in this book (although I've stayed friends with several others). One of the people I lost touch with was Roxy. My crush faded, and I went a little girl-crazy after college, meeting as many women online as I could, going out on dates with them, and fucking as many as would let me. Little did I know one of those women would be the love of my life, and I married her two years after we met.

Social anxiety still plays a role in my life. I think it always will. But I've made progress, and I can confidently say that it plays less of a role in my life now than it did when I first started writing this book.

## Summer of Salvia

I've started a successful career in communications, have a loving family and a beautiful wife. Despite the existential crises I've struggled with, I have a good life. A happy life. It could be a lot worse.

But I also have to admit that ever since I smoked salvia, the thought of what I experienced that night has never been far from my mind. Part of that, I suppose, was driven by my desire to complete this book so I could move on with my life.

But another part of the obsession is driven by my fundamental need to know the truth about what I, and countless others, experienced on salvia.* Human beings have an innate need to search for meaning in life, but salvia seemed to ramp that need up to dangerous levels. It's like I was an ant in an ant farm that escaped, free to explore the outside world for a few minutes before getting scooped up and plopped back into the confines of the farm. We're basically all ants trying to understand the nature of this glass prison we're trapped in.

I can't say I was ever completely satisfied by my conception of reality even before I smoked salvia. I remember driving along a highway one summer when I was nineteen, and marveling at the beautiful expanse of blue sky in front of me, and the majesty of the mountains dominating the landscape. *What is this?* I remember thinking. *What is this world we're in? How is it possible that we exist?*

I think it's normal for people to have thoughts like that from time to time. Prior to smoking salvia, I had those kinds of thoughts plenty of times, but infrequently. I wasn't completely

---

\* And also, in my case, while having intense dissociative episodes and panic attacks on three separate occasions while high on marijuana. Although the episodes felt linked to my experience on *Salvia divinorum*, I'm not convinced they were. But I don't know—perhaps marijuana can sometimes "lift the veil" the same way salvia does.

# Epilogue: Truth

unlike Stuart Mason, who says in his book that before smoking salvia, he believed there "was really one reality that we all shared and collectively participated in." It's what we're taught from birth. Why would any of us question what seems like such an irrefutable truth—one that is constantly reinforced not only by our parents, our education system, and our entire society, but also by our very senses?

When I smoked salvia, that all changed. I wouldn't say I became obsessed with my search for the true nature of our existence, but the question has certainly come to dominate much more of my day-to-day mental energy.

That's not inherently a bad thing. I think it's great for people to explore many different theories and beliefs about the origins of humanity and the nature of the universe and our everyday reality. But even as I explored these questions, I realized I would never know the truth for certain—at least, not until I died.

One of the things that scares me most about death is the thought that, if atheists are correct, we simply cease to exist when we die. I can't stand the thought of never knowing for sure what comes next. If it's nothingness, so be it, but I wish there was a moment just before the end when a little angel lowered its lips to our ears and whispered, "This is it. After this moment, you'll cease to be—forever." I think I could die in peace, then, even knowing I was destined for oblivion.

Although my experience on salvia cast a ton of doubt in me about my religious beliefs and the nature of reality, I still consider myself a Christian. Maybe that says more about the power of childhood religious indoctrination than anything else—about how strongly those early ideas of religion instill themselves deep inside you. But I prefer to think it speaks to the strength and power of faith. Being a Christian hasn't precluded me from exploring many of the philosophical and existential ideas presented in this book and even incorporating some of them into my Christian worldview.

For example, I often think about Bostrom's theory that we may be living in a computer simulation. What's to say we aren't? And what's to say that this simulation wasn't crafted by the majestic hands of some magnificent God who created our world with a grand plan in mind?

Religious skeptics tend to scoff at the idea of a God who takes an interest in every single one of his human creations, and I admit that's an idea that boggles my mind to no end. There's billions of humans currently living on this planet, and countless others have died throughout human history. Does God really care about each one of those souls, individually? It seems like the skeptics are right—that it's impossible.

What gets lost in the debate is that even if our world were constructed to reflect the world that God lives in, that doesn't mean our world, and its physical laws, are exactly the same as in God's world. Just because *our* minds can't comprehend the thought of keeping track of billions of individuals doesn't mean God can't do so with ease.

Take the video game *The Sims*, for example. For those not familiar with the game, it is essentially a simulation of reality, much in line with Bostrom's theory, but on a much cruder scale. In *The Sims*, the player creates characters, called sims, and controls every aspect of their lives, from the houses they live in, to the jobs they work, to the relationships they form. The player can give the characters some degree of autonomy, but can also intervene whenever they wish.

Imagine if the characters in *The Sims* were sentient. Imagine living in their digital world, constrained by the laws put forth by

## Epilogue: Truth

the programmers who made the game. Now imagine that a programmer took the consciousness of one of the sims and uploaded it into the mind of an android. Suddenly, the character from the game has a physical, albeit robotic, body in the "real" world. Can you imagine how mind-blowing it would be for the sim to experience a world infinitely more real than the one he or she was born into? It might be a lot like tripping on salvia.

Imagine all the physical laws in the real world that would differ from the laws they'd experienced in the game world. Time would flow differently. Objects would be made of atoms rather than pixels. The laws that made up the very fabric of their existence would be turned upside down. So why do we think that all the physical laws and properties of our own world would be the same in a higher reality?

If there is some other reality or dimension out there—whether it's been visited by hallucinogen-fueled psychonauts or not—all we can do is speculate about what it may be like. Although some think salvia, LSD, psilocybin mushrooms, mescaline or DMT can give them a peek into the world that awaits us beyond the grave, there's no way for us to know whether these drugs truly lift the veil obscuring reality, or simply offer a mirage painted by a brain gone haywire.

There's only one way to know for sure: to experience death (if there's anything to experience). That's a truth Brett Chidester realized after smoking salvia—a truth that apparently drove him to take drastic and fatal action in an attempt to answer the existential questions that plagued him. I'm not saying it's normal or common for salvia to drive people to commit suicide in search of answers, but I do think, compounded with whatever other issues Chidester may have been dealing with in his life, a salvia-induced existential crisis could have nudged him toward the edge of the proverbial cliff.

Since I took salvia, I've devoted much time to searching for my own answers about the true nature of existence. Though I've learned a lot about the different perspectives on this subject, I'm no closer to knowing with certainty what life is or why we're living it. I'll never stop searching, but ultimately, all I can do is put my faith in Jesus Christ and wait for death.

Whatever your beliefs, that last part is all any of us can do. Maybe that's the true meaning of life. It's a somber thought, perhaps even a depressing one, but it's comforting to think that if we're patient, we'll have all our questions about existence answered.

Either there's nothing on the other side, and we'll never know it, or there's *something*—maybe something terrible, maybe something wonderful, but *something*, nonetheless, that we will get to *know*, to experience. I pray we'll get that opportunity someday—the opportunity to *know*. To have all of our questions about why we're here, about the meaning of life, about God, definitively answered. To have our earthly amnesia cured, and to remember where we come from and why we left in the first place.

Maybe we're all the same entity experiencing the world through billions of different eyes. A few days after my salvia trip, when a whirlwind of strange ideas were still flying through my head, I had the thought that maybe God had taken the cosmic equivalent of LSD, and the world that we were born into is His hallucination. Maybe, I thought, we're all pieces of the same shattered God, each of us representing some tiny aspect of the deity's celestial psyche. Maybe when we awaken from this life we'll find ourselves reclaiming our divinity while trying to make sense of the billions of lives we've just lived. Maybe the memories of those lives will stick with us through our eternal adventures,

## Epilogue: Truth

and impact the choices we make going forward.

Or maybe we'll be quickly forgotten, dismissed as a silly, fleeting hallucination of no consequence.

We'll wait and see. It's literally all we can do.

# Appendix

I HOPE THIS BOOK HAS GIVEN YOU A BETTER UNDERSTANDING of *Salvia divinorum*, but the fact is, this book barely scratches the surface of what this plant can do and what it means to the people who do it—from the Mazatec Indians, to modern-day psychonauts, to risk-taking, would-be YouTube stars.

If I've managed to pique your interest in salvia and you want to know more, you are certainly welcome to perform a Google search for more information. But I've already done a lot of research and found some of the best resources on salvia, both online and offline. So if you're hungry for more, check out these websites, books, films and other sources for information on salvia.

### WEBSITES

**Summer of Salvia.** *Summerofsalvia.com*. We'll get the shameless plug out of the way first—this is my own website. I occasionally post articles on *Salvia divinorum*, as well as information about my book, including occasional giveaways.

**Sage Wisdom.** *Sagewisdom.org.* Daniel Siebert's Sage Wisdom website is *the* go-to source for information on *Salvia divinorum* on the web.

**Salvia.net.** *Salvia.net.* This website has a section with dozens of trip reports written by people who have used *Salvia divinorum.*

**Erowid.** *Erowid.org/plants/salvia/salvia.shtml.* This website has a lot of information on *Salvia divinorum*, including trip reports.

**A World Out of Mind.** *Salviaspace.blogspot.com.* "Saint Brian the Godless" blogs about his experiences on *Salvia divinorum.* The blog is updated somewhat sporadically; Saint Brian's Twitter account is more active: @AWorldOutOfMind.

**Xka Pastora.** *http://xkapastora.org/en/.* Xka Pastora is a center for research and ethnobotanical conservation of *Salvia divinorum*, according to its website.

### Films

**Salvia Documentary.** *Salviadocumentary.com.* At the time of this writing, this documentary has not yet been released, but it should be soon. Check the website for updates on a release date.

**Salvia Movie.** *Salviamovie.com, facebook.com/thesalviamovie.* This film, separate from the above film, also has not been released at the time of this writing. Check the website for updates.

## Appendix

**Salvia: Sage of the Seers.** Available on YouTube at https://www.youtube.com/watch?v=7h1uq-T1qUI.

**Sacred Weeds, Salvia divinorum segment.** Available on YouTube at https://www.youtube.com/watch?v=0T_x__Xh4Ew

### Books on Salvia

*Salvia Divinorum: Doorway to Thought-Free Awareness*, by J.D. Arthur. ISBN: 978-1594773471.

*Salvia Divinorum Growers Guide: How to Grow Salvia Divinorum*, by Richard Glen Boire. ASIN: B00U6HW2EY.

*Salvia Divinorum: The Sage of Seers*, by Ross Heaven. ISBN: 978-1782792529.

*Salvia Divinorum: A User's Guide*, by Alfred Freeman. ASIN: B00QVWCRZM.

*Salvia Divinorum: Shamanic Plant Medicine*, by Shaahin Cheyene. ASIN: B001UQ5HVA.

*Shamanic Quest for the Spirit of Salvia: The Divinatory, Visionary, and Healing Powers of the Sage of the Seers*, by Ross Heaven. ISBN: 978-1620550007.

*Salvia Divinorum: Reality of Life and Death*, by Stuart Mason. ISBN: 9781447760931. (Available only at Lulu.com.)

*Sage Spirit: Salvia Divinorum and the Entheogenic Experience*, by
Martin. W. Ball. ISBN: 9780615157085.

*Salvia Divinorum: A Correlated Experience*, by Matt Schmitz.
ASIN: B01C34PQMW.

*Salvinorin: The Psychedelic Essence of Salvia Divinorum*, by
D.M. Turner. (This book is out of print, but an HTML-based
web version is available at lavondyss.com/donut/scov.html).

## Magazines

*The Ethneogen Review*. *Entheogenreview.com*

### Books on Ideas Linked to Salvia

*Is There Life After Death?*, by Anthony Peake. ISBN: 978-1848372993.

*The Holographic Universe*, by Michael Talbot. ISBN: 978-0062014108.

*I Am a Strange Loop*, by Douglas Hofstadter. ISBN: 978-0465030798.

*Faith Awakened*, by Grace Bridges. ISBN: 978-0986451706.

*Arena*, by Karen Hancock. ISBN: 978-0764226311.

# Appendix

Everything ever written by Philip K. Dick.

Everything ever written by Alan W. Watts.

## Movies on Ideas Linked to Salvia

*The Matrix*
*The Truman Show*
*Groundhog Day*
*Total Recall*
*Vanilla Sky*
*ExistenZ*
*Synecdoche, New York*
*The Thirteenth Floor*
*World on a Wire*
*Inception*
*Waking Life*
*What the Bleep Do We Know?!*
*Dark City*

## TV Shows on Ideas Linked to Salvia

*Rick and Morty* (particularly the season two episode, *Mortynight Run*)
*Dollhouse*

## Short Stories on Ideas Related to Salvia

**The Egg**, by Andy Weir. Available on Weir's website: *Galactanet.com/oneoff/theegg_mod.html*.

# Summer of Salvia

## Where to Buy Salvia Divinorum Products

There are countless shops online offering dried salvia leaves or salvinorin A extracts, in addition to other salvia products. Here are some of them. Many local tobacco stores and head shops also carry salvia products.

Take this information with the caveat that I do not endorse the use of *Salvia divinorum*, and if you choose to purchase or use salvia, or any kind of *Salvia divinorum* product, you do so at your own risk. I take no responsibility for your actions, and this section is in no way any kind of endorsement of any of the sites listed or any of the products they sell.

### For Dried Leaves and Extracts

**Sage Wisdom Botanicals.** *Sagewisdombotanicals.com.*

**Arena Ethnobotanicals.** *Arenaethnobotanicals.com*

**Salvia Dragon.** *Salviadragon.com*

### For Live Plants

**Sage Wisdom Botanicals.** *Sagewisdombotanicals.com.*

**Mazatec Garden.** *Mazatecgarden.com.*

**Botanical Spirit Shop.** *Botanicalspirit.com*

### For Seeds

# Appendix

*Note: Salvia divinorum rarely grows via seed. Keep in mind that even if you purchase Salvia divinorum seeds, you may not end up with a viable Salvia divinorum plant.*

**Sage Wisdom Botanicals.** *Sagewisdombotanicals.com.*

## For Tincture

**Sage Wisdom Botanicals.** *Sagewisdombotanicals.com.*

**Avalon Magic Plants.** *Avalonmagicplants.com.*

**Salvia Hut.** *Salviahut.com.*

# About the Author

There's not much to tell—Jason Cole is a pseudonym, remember?—but I'll throw you a bone: Here's the story of how I chose my pseudonym.

The working pen name I used when I first started this book sucked. It was just a placeholder until I thought of something better.

Long before I started writing this book—when I was in high school, in fact—I frequently used MSN instant messenger to talk to my friends. This was before text messaging was big. Instant messaging was popular because you could hold conversations with a dozen of your friends at once.

One of the features of MSN messenger was that you could change your display name to whatever you wanted, as often as you wanted. People had a lot of fun with this, making all kinds of pop culture references and whatnot in their display name.

One day, I logged in and decided to change my display name

to something completely random. I literally just ran my fingers across the keyboard a couple times and ended up with something completely random: elocnosaj. "Good enough," I said.

A couple minutes later, one of my friends messaged me. "Who's Jason Cole?" he asked.

"Huh?" I replied.

"Jason Cole," he repeated. "Your display name is Jason Cole spelled backward."

I was flabbergasted. I explained that my display name was just a random string of letters, but he didn't believe me—he thought I'd done it on purpose and was being cheeky or something. I was amazed that the random string of letters I'd hit ended up spelling a name backward.

Years later, when I was trying to think of a good pseudonym, this memory popped into my head. Instantly, I knew I'd found my pseudonym. Jason Cole. It seemed preordained. And for a book discussing the mystic nature of a powerful hallucinogenic drug, it was perfect.

I suppose maybe there's more that you'd like to know "about" me as the author of this book, but the fact is, I divulge a lot about myself in the book itself. So sit back, read it if you haven't already, and enjoy learning more about me than many of my own friends and family know.

One last thing: If you made it all the way to the end of this book, you must have been invested, even if you ultimately ended up disliking it. Whether you loved the book, hated it, or land somewhere in the middle, it would mean a lot if you'd take a moment to leave a review on Amazon or whatever other bookseller you may have purchased the book from. Writing a book is an arduous task, but reviews help provide validation for all the hard work, and help other interested readers find out about the book.

## About the Author

If you want to keep in touch with me—I may have a few more books in me yet—you can do so online:

**Website:** summerofsalvia.com

**Email:** summerofsalvia@gmail.com

**Facebook:** facebook.com/SummerOfSalvia

**Twitter:** twitter.com/SummerOfSalvia

**Google Plus:** tinyurl.com/JasonColeGooglePlus

# Notes

*Author's Note: Due to this book's structure—the first half is an autobiographical narrative, and therefore cites no sources other than my memory—there are no notes for chapters 1-14.*

*Additionally, many of these sources are online and, given the ever-changing nature of the internet, by the time you read this, the links may be outdated. If you attempt to view a source and find that the link no longer works, try using the Internet Archive at* https://archive.org/web/. *The site archives web pages so even if they go dead, a historical representation of the page is preserved for posterity's sake. Not all websites get archived, but many do, so it's certainly worth looking to see if a dead link has been preserved.*

## Chapter 15: Early History

1 Ott, Jonathan. "Ethnopharmacognosy and Human Pharmacology of Salvia divinorum and Salvinorin A." Sage Wisdom.

Accessed 2017. http://www.sagewisdom.org/ott2.html.

2 Ibid.

3 Whitcomb, Sean. "Salvia divinorum, Herb of Mary, the Shepherdess." Southern Illinois University Carbondale / Ethnobotanical Leaflets. May 15, 1998. Accessed 2017. http://opensiuc.lib.siu.edu/cgi/viewcontent.cgi?article=1368&context=ebl.

4 Valdes, Leander J., III, Jose Luis Diaz, and Ara G. Paul. "Ethnopharmacology of Ska Maria Pastora (Part 2)." IAmShaman.com. July 10, 1982. Accessed 2017. https://www.iamshaman.com/salvia/mazatecs.htm.

5 "Salvia divinorum." CESAR: Center for Substance Abuse Research. Accessed 2017. http://www.cesar.umd.edu/cesar/drugs/salvia.asp?a_aid=3598aabf#history.

6 Sullum, Jacob. "The Salvia Ban Wagon." Reason.com. December 2009. Accessed 2017. http://reason.com/archives/2009/11/19/the-salvia-ban-wagon/singlepage.

7 Horowitz, Michael. "An Interview with Albert Hofmann." Erowid. Originally published in High Times. 1976. Accessed 2017. https://erowid.org/culture/characters/hofmann_albert/hofmann_albert_interview1.shtml.

8 Siebert, Daniel. "The history of the first Salvia divinorum plants cultivated outside of Mexico." Sage Wisdom. 2003. Accessed 2017. http://www.sagewisdom.org/salviahistory.html.

9 Kabil, Ahmed. "This Mexican medicine woman hipped America to magic mushrooms, with the help of a bank executive." Timeline. January 4, 2017. Accessed 2017. https://timeline.com/with-the-help-of-a-bank-executive-this-mexican-medicine-woman-hipped-america-to-magic-mushrooms-c41f866bbf37.

10 Beyer, Steve. "The Tragedy of Maria Sabina." Singing to the Plants. February 17, 2008. Accessed 2017. http://www.singingto-

# NOTES

theplants.com/2008/02/tragedy-of-maria-sabina/.

11  Wasson, R. Gordon. "Seeking the Magic Mushroom." Imaginaria.org. Originally published in LIFE Magazine. June 10, 1957. Accessed 2017. http://www.imaginaria.org/wasson/life.htm.

12  Beyer, "The Tragedy of Maria Sabina."

## CHAPTER 16: MODERN HISTORY

1  Cambron, Melisa. "A comparison of historical and current use of Salvia divinorum in the United States and Mexico." Lake Forest College Eukaryon. March 2016. https://www.lakeforest.edu/live/news/6656-a-comparison-of-historical-and-current-use-of.

2  Wu, Li-Tzy, George E. Woody, Chongming Yang, Jih-Heng Li, and Dan G. Blazer. "Recent national trends in Salvia divinorum use and substance-use disorders among recent and former Salvia divinorum users compared with nonusers." Substance Abuse and Rehabilitation, 2011. Accessed 2017. https://www.ncbi.nlm.nih.gov/pmc/articles/PMC3122136/.

3  Gleiter, Christoph H., R. Bucheler, P. Schwoerer, and I. Gaertner. "Use of Nonprohibited Hallucinogenic Plants: Increasing Relevance for Public health?" Sage Wisdom. Originally published in Pharmacopsychiatry. 2005. Accessed 2017. http://www.sagewisdom.org/bucheleretal.pdf.

4  Miller, Bryan Lee, John M. Stogner, David N. Khey, Ronald L. Akers, John Boman, and O. Hayden Griffin. "Magic Mint, The Internet, and Peer Associations: A Test of Social Learning Theory Using Patterns of Salvia Divinorum Use." Sage Journals, Journal of Drug Issues. July 1, 2011. Accessed 2017. http://journals.sagepub.com/doi/abs/10.1177/002204261104100301.

5  "Miley Cyrus: Bong Video Partying with a Bong." TMZ. December 12, 2010. Accessed 2017. http://www.tmz.com/2010/12/10/miley-cyrus-video-bong-hit-smoking-salvia-

herb-pyschedelic-birthday-party-hannah-montana/.

6 Mapes, Jillian. "Miley Cyrus Opens Up About Salvia Bong Hit." Billboard. February 9, 2011. Accessed 2017. http://www.billboard.com/articles/news/473147/miley-cyrus-opens-up-about-salvia-bong-hit.

7 "'I'll Have What She's Having.'" TMZ. December 13, 2010. Accessed 2017. http://www.tmz.com/2010/12/13/miley-cyrus-salvia-divinorum-bong-herbal-drug-smoking-video-head-shops-sales-increase-smoke-shops/.

8 Spring, Tom. "'Salvia Killed My Son,' Says Mother." PCWorld. February 1, 2009. Accessed 2017. http://www.pcworld.com/article/158104/Salvia_kills.html.

9 "Drug Fact Sheets." DEA.gov. Accessed 2017. https://www.dea.gov/druginfo/factsheets.shtml.

10 Siebert, Daniel. "The Legal Status of Salvia Divinorum." Sage Wisdom. August 12, 2015. Accessed 2017. http://www.sagewisdom.org/legalstatus.html.

11 Sack, Kevin and McDonald, Brent. "Popularity of a Hallucinogen May Thwart Its Medical Uses." New York Times. September 8, 2008. Accessed 2017. http://www.nytimes.com/2008/09/09/us/09salvia.html.

12 "Roosevelt Island Resident Dies After Jumping Off Apartment Balcony At Manhattan Park's 10 River Road." Roosevelt Islander Online. March 6, 2011. Accessed 2017. http://rooseveltislander.blogspot.com/2011/03/roosevelt-island-resident-dies-after.html.

13 Roth, Jamie. "Man Smoked Salvia Before Jumping to Death, Family Says." ABC 7 WABC-TV. March 8, 2011. Accessed 2017. http://abc7ny.com/archive/8001683/.

# Notes

14 "Teenager's tragic fall while on a 'legal high.'" Hastings & St Leonards Observer. September 3, 2011. Accessed 2017. http://www.hastingsobserver.co.uk/news/teenager-s-tragic-fall-while-on-a-legal-high-1-3021747.

15 "Arizona Congresswoman Giffords shot; doctors 'optimistic' about recovery chances." The Arizona Republic. January 8, 2011. Accessed 2017. http://archive.azcentral.com/news/articles/2011/01/08/20110108arizona-giffords-brk.html.

16 "Rep. Giffords shot, judge and 5 others killed at Tucson event." Arizona Daily Star. January 8, 2011. Accessed 2017. http://tucson.com/news/local/rep-giffords-shot-judge-and-others-killed-at-tucson-event/article_88b4b436-1b53-11e0-8354-001cc4c002e0.html.

17 Sulzberger, A.G., and Jennifer Medina. "Shooting Suspect Had Been Known to Use Potent, and Legal, Hallucinogen." New York Times. January 17, 2011. Accessed 2017. http://www.nytimes.com/2011/01/18/us/18salvia.html.

18 Sullum, Jacob. "The Salvia Ban Wagon." Reason.com. December 2009. Accessed 2017. http://reason.com/archives/2009/11/19/the-salvia-ban-wagon/singlepage.

## Chapter 17: Science

1 Cohn, Meredith. "Hopkins researchers study effects of salvia." The Baltimore Sun. December 10, 2010. Accessed 2017. https://web.archive.org/web/20160731182008/http://articles.baltimoresun.com/2010-12-10/health/bs-hs-hallucinogen-salvia-20101210_1_salvia-new-drug-hopkins-researchers.

2 "Brain's Reaction to Potent Hallucinogen Salvia Explored." Science Daily. April 28, 2008. Accessed 2017. https://www.sciencedaily.com/releases/2008/04/080428120701.htm.

3 Ortega, A., JF Blount, and PD Manchand. "Salvinorin, A New trans-Neoclerodane Diterpene from Salvia divinorum (Labiatae)." Erowid. Originally published in the Journal of the Chemical Society, Perkins Transactions I. March 3, 1982. Accessed 2017. https://erowid.org/plants/salvia/salvia_journal4.shtml.

4 O'Neill, Tony. "What's So Scary About Salvia?" The Fix. May 16, 2011. Accessed 2017. https://www.thefix.com/content/salvia?page=all.

5 Lewis, Marc. "The True Self: Unveiled by Dissociative Drugs? Part 1." Psychology Today. November 21, 2011. Accessed 2017. https://www.psychologytoday.com/blog/addicted-brains/201111/the-true-self-unveiled-dissociative-drugs-part-1.

6 Turner, D.M. "Salvinorin: The Psychedelic Essence of Salvia Divinorum." Erowid. 1996. Accessed 2017. https://erowid.org/library/books_online/salvinorin/disc.shtml.

7 Siebert, Daniel. "Salvinorin A: The Breakthrough." Sage Wisdom. Originally Published in the Journal of Ethnopharmacology. 1994. Accessed 2017. http://www.sagewisdom.org/salvexpe.html.

8 Sack, Kevin and McDonald, Brent. "Popularity of a Hallucinogen May Thwart Its Medical Uses." New York Times. September 8, 2008. Accessed 2017. http://www.nytimes.com/2008/09/09/us/09salvia.html.

9 Kivell, Bronwyn M., Amy WM Ewald, and Thomas E. Prisinzano. "Salvinorin A analogs and other kappa opioid receptor compounds as treatments for cocaine abuse." Adv Pharmacol, January 1, 2015. Accessed 2017. https://www.ncbi.nlm.nih.gov/pmc/articles/PMC4128345/.

10 RG, Dos Santos, Crippa JA, Machado-de-Sousa JP, and Hallak JE. "Salvinorin a and related compounds as therapeutic drugs for psychostimulant-related disorders." Current drug abuse

reviews, 2014. Accessed 2017. https://www.ncbi.nlm.nih.gov/pubmed/25563442.

11 James, Susan Donaldson. "Salvia Studies Hold Promise for Addiction." ABC News. January 3, 2010. Accessed 2017. http://abcnews.go.com/Health/Wellness/salvia-study-shows-hope-addiction-alzheimers-pain-therapies/story?id=12364682.

12 Siebert, Daniel. "How to Obtain Effects From Smoked Salvia Divinorum." Sage Wisdom. May 27, 2002. Accessed 2017. http://www.sagewisdom.org/smokeadvice.html.

13 Siebert, Daniel. "The *Salvia divinorum* User's Guide." Sage Wisdom. April 17, 2010. Accessed 2017. http://www.sagewisdom.org/usersguide.html.

14 Ibid.

15 "Usage." Salvia World. 2010. Accessed 2017. http://www.salvia-world.com/usage.html.

## Chapter 18: Philosophy

1 Bostrom, Nick. "Are You Living in a Computer Simulation?" Simulation-Argument.com. Originally published in Philosophical Quarterly. 2003. Accessed 2017. http://www.simulation-argument.com/simulation.html.

2 Loria, Kevin. "Neil deGrasse Tyson thinks there's a 'very high' chance the universe is just a simulation." Business Insider. December 23, 2016. Accessed 2017. http://www.businessinsider.com/neil-degrasse-tyson-thinks-the-universe-might-be-a-simulation-2016-12.

3 Rothman, Joshua. "What Are the Odds We Are Living in a Computer Simulation?" The New Yorker. June 9, 2016. Accessed 2017. http://www.newyorker.com/books/joshua-rothman/what-are-the-odds-we-are-living-in-a-computer-simulation.

4 Rice, Doyle. "Mind blown: The entire universe could be a hologram." USA Today. January 30, 2017. Accessed 2017. https://www.usatoday.com/story/tech/sciencefair/2017/01/30/universe-hologram-illusion/97249856/.

5 Mason, Stuart. *Salvia Divinorum: Reality of Life and Death.* Retrieved via Google Books: http://tinyurl.com/RealityLifeAndDeath.

6 Stu Mas. (Stuart Mason's YouTube Channel). https://www.youtube.com/user/tvsuat.

7 Williams, Rhiannon. "Virtual reality for chickens: fair or fowl?" The Telegraph. May 16, 2014. Accessed 2017. http://www.telegraph.co.uk/technology/news/10835849/Virtual-reality-for-chickens-fair-or-fowl.html.

## Chapter 19: Religion

1 "Eternal Return." Wikipedia. Accessed 2017. https://en.wikipedia.org/wiki/Eternal_return.

2 "Does my life repeat." Salvia-trip.net. December 16, 2011. Accessed 2017. http://www.salvia-trip.net/exp/does_my_life_repeat-e1507/.

3 "Maya." Encyclopædia Britannica. Accessed 2017. https://www.britannica.com/topic/maya-Indian-philosophy.

4 Crumb, Robert. "The Religious Experience of Philip K. Dick." Philip K. Dick Fan Site. Accessed 2017. http://www.philipkdickfans.com/resources/miscellaneous/the-religious-experience-of-philip-k-dick-by-r-crumb-from-weirdo-17/.

5 Dick, Philip K. *The Exegesis of Philip K. Dick.* Boston: Houghton Mifflin Harcourt: 2011.

6 Dick, Philip K. Excerpt from *The Exegesis of Philip K. Dick.*

# Notes

Montalk.net. Accessed 2017. http://montalk.net/PKD_principles.html.

7 "Gnosticism, Christianity, and Sophia." Kenyon College Department of Religious Studies. Accessed 2017. http://www2.kenyon.edu/Depts/Religion/Projects/Reln91/Gender/Gnosticism.htm.

8 Dick, Phillip K. *VALIS*. Accessed 2017. New York: Mariner Books: 2011. Retrieved on Google Books: http://tinyurl.com/PKDGnosticVALIS.

## Chapter 20: Conclusions

1 "Comboning. [sic] Quantum physics with my many salvia divinorum experiences." Reddit. March 19, 2017. Accessed 2017. https://www.reddit.com/r/Salvia/comments/60ca73/comboning_quantum_physics_with_my_many_salvia/.

2 "Salvia pulling effect." Shroomery.org. January 20, 2013. Accessed 2017. https://www.shroomery.org/forums/showflat.php/Number/17578444.

3 "Being pulled.." Salvia-trip.net. September 11, 2009. Accessed 2017. http://www.salvia-trip.net/exp/being_pulled..-e1119/.

4 Cumberdale, Hubert. "Goodbye Reality, Goodbye Universe." Erowid. November 26, 2011. Accessed 2017. https://erowid.org/experiences/exp.php?ID=86484.

5 "Salvia Divinorum - Semi-experienced & a First Timer - Into Deep." Bluelight.org. Dec. 23, 2011. Accessed 2017. http://www.bluelight.org/vb/threads/603163-Salvia-Divinorum-Semi-experienced-amp-a-First-Timer-Into-Deep.

6 Vulpine. "Reality is a Five Spoked Wheel." Erowid. October 30, 2007. Accessed 2017. https://erowid.org/experiences/exp.php?ID=45012.

www.ingramcontent.com/pod-product-compliance
Lightning Source LLC
Chambersburg PA
CBHW020359080526
44584CB00014B/1083